Way, Way Beyond

The Story Behind

Janis Joplin's Psychedelic
PORSCHE 356

and 49 other Highly Entertaining Tales
From the World of Rare and Exotic Car Collecting

Wallace Wyss

Enthusiast Books

Visit www.enthusiastbooks.com

To contact us or request a catalog, go to www.enthusiastbooks.com or call us at 1-715-381-9755.

Library of Congress Control Number: 1-4032271751

ISBN-13: 978-1-58388-343-4
ISBN-10: 1-58388-343-6

Printed in The United States of America

Way, Way Beyond "Barn Finds"…

The Story Behind

Janis Joplin's Psychedelic
PORSCHE 356

and 49 other Highly Entertaining Tales
From the World of Rare and Exotic Car Collecting

Table of Contents

Guest Forward

It turns out, before I met Wallace Wyss, I had read many of his articles. Now that I have seen his *Incredible Barn Finds* series, I have to say that, on numerous postwar classics, with perhaps a couple of minor differences, we are of the same mind.

For instance, in the Concorso Italiano events in Monterey, we celebrate the low cost Italian car, such as the Fiat X1/9, just as much as the fancier more exotic thoroughbreds such as Ferrari, Lamborghini and Maserati. Wallace restricts his coverage in the book series to cars now worth more than $100,000 when restored. To include cars more accessibly priced readers would need a strong back to hoist a tome undoubtedly weighing in excess of eight pounds.

Both of us enjoy prototypes that are put on the road. This includes cars such as the Bertone Pirana, the Maserati Boomerang, the Alfa Canguro, and the BAT Alfas. Wallace and I applaud, in our own way, the indefatigable efforts of barn finders who search out these cars and rescue them from the crusher, so we who missed them the first time in their original show careers can finally enjoy them.

I notice in the series that Wallace is paying a bit more attention, as he adds the "cult of personality". That is to say, while appreciating the shape of the car, and its performance and engineering, Wallace is adding a bit more on the incredible people that envisioned these cars. Not so much that the personality of the car's creator dominates his stories, but when Wallace has insight into what they were thinking, he gives it full exposure—people like Tom Tjaarda, Sergio Scaglietti, Marcello Gandini, and Raymond

Loewy. Wallace believes knowledge of the creator makes seeing the cars much more enjoyable.

Another thing we share is the love for the forgotten marques. Cars such as the Apollo, the Italia, and so forth, usually hybrids of one marque with another marque's engine, which in the past got shunted aside by collectors in the mad rush to buy thoroughbreds. Thoroughbreds are defined as a car where the engine is made by the same people that built the car. At Concorso Italiano 2013 in Monterey, we highlighted the Apollo, designed by an American, but built in Italy. Prior to that time most people had never heard of the Apollo.

We also both like Italian cars with American V8 engines--Bizzarrinis, Iso Grifos, Ghia 450/SS, Dual Ghias for, I suspect, the same reason. We have a recurring nightmare our exotic car will break down somewhere west of Laramie and would like to be able to go to the nearest auto parts store and buy a coil for a Ford, Chevy or Chrysler.

Concorso Italiano will continue to evolve, as our core group expresses their desires for more background, more information on the cars that they see before them. On event day, our emcee talks from dawn to dusk in that regard, but we're augmenting his patter with more incisive articles in the event magazine. I'm hoping you'll enjoy Wallace's book which gives you insight into why some of these cars were created.

Tom McDowell
President, Concorso Italiano
Seattle, Washington

Author's Introduction

Welcome to the latest volume in the *Incredible Barn Finds* series (earlier ones are available by going to www.enthusiastbooks.com.)

I have noticed some trends, now that I have chronicled 200 collector cars found in unusual ways. First is that some have had the wrong body on them for awhile, which meant collectors looking for a certain model didn't realize that oddball had underneath it the object of their desire.

The second trend is that not all collector cars ascend in value equally. Some brands seem to be stuck like a racehorse tied to the starting gate. Before you leap into one of these "unknown" appreciators, it's best to go to every car auction website, read each auction result, to see if they are showing signs of appreciating yet. Say, for instance DeTomaso Panteras. For decades they resold at around $25,000 partly because so many owners had hot rodded them. But now that the much rarer DeTomaso Mangustas have soared above $200,000, that has pulled Panteras up to at least $60,000 and certain rare models not imported to America by Ford, like the GT-5 and GT5-S, might be cracking the $200,000 barrier.

The third trend is that there is a change in head space on what's acceptable to take to a car meet. At one time, cars still being restored weren't even considered. But now even at Pebble Beach, the most famous venue for concours display, there is a "survivor" class where it's OK to enter a car that is dented, has the paint flaking off, etc. as long as it represents that car as it originally was produced.

And then here is a new kind of car show, a very informal

un-structured one called "Cars 'n Coffee" that usually takes place in a shopping center parking lot. There's no entering in a formal sense, you just show up, buy a cuppa coffee and walk around talking to people about why they bought this and that car.

A fourth trend, one that threatens authentically restored cars (though I think there is room in the tent for everybody) is the advent of the "resto-mod" which I define as restored on the outside to look relatively stock but with a modern day drivetrain underneath. Now there those purists who will decry this trend saying "How can this '57 Corvette represent what it was like to drive a '57 Corvette if it's got a modern engine and independent rear suspension, etc.?" I say, from their standpoint, they are right but some owners want the looks of an old car, but don't want the plodding old engine, the solid axle suspension, the drum brakes etc. I purposely didn't include any resto-mods in here because I can't say they have as much appreciation potential as an original car still with its original type engine, original suspension, etc. They are cars bought just for fun so it's best not to get too financially buried in them.

A Different Reason to be an Old Car Expert

And in this book, different from the preceding three volumes, for the first time I discuss merchandising the labors of all your hard work in finding cars, researching them, photographing them and the like. I am involved with a thoroughbred ranching operation today so don't have any budget of my own for collector cars. But it doesn't mean I've lost interest. No, every weekend you will find me at a concours, a cars 'n coffee or something in between. I'm always looking but not just for candidates for these books, or for my own garage. I'm looking to add to my knowledge base because once again, I find my knowledge, my accumulated facts set into little packets of pictures and descriptions, is worth something.

Back in the 1980s I was almost a full time barn finder, finding Rolls Royces, Bentleys , Ferraris, Bizzarrinis, and the like and had clients I was buying cars for in New York and other States. Then when the internet became common I found it difficult to keep from being "claim jumped" as I sent information to buyers on cars I found. So I stayed away from scouting until just recently when I came across two collections that I knew I just had to get the word out on while they were still available. I was able to package the information in a way that told prospective clients what the cars were but not *where* they were. Now many I told of the information being available said "I'll pay you a commission when I successfully buy it" but I can't wait years (or decades) until that happens. For a much smaller price, I sell the info now and it might be years before I hear what they did with that info. I'm not saying you could make a living at being a tipster, I'm just saying merchandising the info is partial justification for all the hours you are putting into finding cars and cataloging information on them.

Another type of car you won' find here is replicas. True, there are some so well made like the Safir GT40 (built with permission from Ford). Those tripled in value since they were new. But cars like replica fiberglass Porsche Speedsters, they don't go up, they just stay at what you bought them at, but nevertheless can be a lot of fun. I can even argue in that car's case, it's a good "scout" car to drive around as eventually someone will say "I got one of those at home--one of the originals." That's when you say "Would you consider selling it?" Then you pay the price for that in any condition and dump the replica because here's where a rhinestone led you to a diamond!

You'll note I don't discuss restoration, and that's on purpose because this series is about the hunt-- finding the car. Sometimes it is not restored, just sold on down the road. (Read the last chapter for tips on how not to buy more than you can handle) I also don't give a Buyer's Guide on any make or model. That's because I imagine there a fair number of you who didn't buy that Speedster or whatever because it had a replacement engine or any of the other sins such Buyer's Guides warn you about, but now that Porsche Speedsters are $170,000, you remember that one you turned down because the Buyer's Guide told you not to buy it for some reason back when it was only $7000!

So Buyer's Guide advice is easily rendered useless by subsequent appreciation.

So here it is—another series of reports from guys who took the plunge..enjoy.

Wallace Wyss
Chino, California

Chapter 1
The Hudson River Submarine
(1967 427 Cobra)
Hey, even junkyards get real Cobras...

The lesson in this story is that it pays to have friends. The lucky guy that bought a smashed 427 Cobra, had a friend who had a junkyard. The friend knew he liked Fords and when he had a wrecked car for sale with a Cobra engine, he called his buddy Sam.

Now the big question is: how did a 427 Cobra, once the most fearsome car on American roads, get to the bottom of the Hudson River?

I'll start at the beginning. It was near the start of spring, on March 3, 1968, on a Sunday afternoon when a Rangoon red 427 Cobra was stolen from a parking lot, reportedly at a nearby technical college.

The Cobra, for those of you unfamiliar with the model, was a lightweight sports car devised by failed chicken farmer turned race driver Carroll Shelby. He started out with a small block version and then graduated to a humongous 7-liter version that could go 0 to 60 mph in 4.2 seconds.

It was a fearsome car one that even its builder, Carroll Shelby, told me candidly "could kill you in a second." Anyway some miscreant stole one, perhaps in Schenectady and began driving hell-for-leather East at rush hour. The miscreant hit a woman crossing the street, killing her, and sped on. Then the driver began to worry that the car would be easily spotted, not only because it was a red Cobra, but because of the now crushed fender. He saw a canal (that was part of the Hudson River) and drove it up to the edge, got out of the car and pushed it in.

He got clean away. The student who owned the car was paid off by the insurance company, probably to the tune of close to its original price of $6,500. But 13 months later, a dredger

dredging the canal hit something bulky. Too bulky to just sweep away, so a diver was sent down to see what the immovable obstacle was and found the Cobra, much the worse for wear for a car with only 7,777 miles on the odometer.

They tried to hook a line on it and lift it up but the line broke so they lowered a bucket on it and picked it up, and that did most of the damage up until they dragged it up on shore and did some more damage, so much so that when it went to a local junkyard it was at first unidentified. Then the junkyard owner noticed it had a 427 Ford engine, a prized engine among racing folk seeing as how this same engine powered NASCAR stock cars. So he called Sam Prock, a local who knew Fords and who had a repair facility. Sam had worked at Hickey Ford in downtown Albany and knew what a Cobra was. But this one had been pretty savaged. Still it was worth buying just for the engine so he towed it home until he could figure out if he wanted to keep it.

He eventually, among the twisted body panels, found the serial number CSX3184. With that he was able to trace down the car's owner, and found out it was owned by the insurance company.

After seeing pictures of the shambles, they didn't want it back. So for the princely sum of $370, he became the owner of a pile of rubble that was once the most fearsome car in America. Money was so tight for him at that time that he had to pay the car off in installments of $20 a month. He couldn't get around to it immediately, what with a growing family and growing business, but began buying the parts—like the eggshell- thin aluminum body panels—that he would need to restore it.

Eventually he met some New York State Police detectives. They said it had been in a hit and run. They even came and got a paint sample to see if it was the same car and that sample did indeed identify it. Unfortunately there were no clues to the driver.

The chassis (in those days some cars still had separate frames) was more together than the body, but he had to repair the frame tubes that had hit the cement dock as it was pushed off into the water.

By 1985, the rescuer was able to start putting it together when he bought an old farm with a chicken coop to house it and had room to work on it. The engine was rebuilt and tested and produced its original 450 hp.

In 2007 he drove the car for the first time and started making appearances at local car shows. The nickname for the car was "the Hudson River submarine. "

By that time auction prices for 427 Cobras were close to half a million dollars (have since reached a million) and, as far as I know, it hasn't been put up for sale but this remains a significant barn find.

Lesson learned? Learn the meaning of the phrase "Hail fellow, well met." Be chummy with everyone, buy that junkyard owner a cold brew on a hot day, or a warm drink on a cold day etc. Tell him what cars you covet and maybe, just maybe when he gets that car that sounds like your dream car, he'll call you first...

Chapter 2
MENAGE A TROIS
(1966 Ferrari 365P Tre-Posti Speciale)
A wild idea, bought new by a gigolo who met a very sad end indeed...

Back in the '60s, Enzo Ferrari was still being a stubborn old man. Oh, on the race cars he had begrudgingly approved going mid-engined for better handling and aerodynamics. But for street cars, he still preferred to have the engine in front.

Nevertheless in the mid-Sixties two special Ferraris were built on what was called a "recovered" 365P chassis by some, leading one to suspect they were old race cars. But this particular car, chassis 8971, was not a race car first. It was a purpose-built chassis. It is said to be one of Sergio Pininfarina's first designs.

It was an odd-looking duck, oh, very refined compared to a race car, but it was very low and very wide, and something unexpected—it seemed years ahead of its time.

One source says both cars were ordered by Fiat boss Gianni

Agnelli, and that one even went on display prematurely at the 1966 Paris Motor Show without its full running gear on Pininfarina's stand.

Now if you're expecting a full race car, as fast as the 365P race car, this was not it, it was tamed down some, the engine throttled down to 380 hp. It was mostly conceived of by Pininfarina as a styling exercise to show that, yes, Signor Ferrari, a mid-engined car *can* be as refined as a front engine car. This one boasted a unique three-seat design with the steering wheel in the middle. Brockbank, the British cartoonist, pictured it with a race driver behind the wheel in the middle and two women fighting with him on either side. (that doesn't make *menage a-trois* look so good…)

It is thought that a center wheel gives a high level of visibility to the driver and maximizes interior space. At any rate, decades later, McLaren designer Gordon Murray copied the idea for his F1 road car.

The *Tre Posti* ("three seater") is said to have tested out many ideas that were used on the Dino prototypes shown in 1965. It might be considered the grand-daddy of the Dino 206/246 production cars.

SHOW CAREER

The car was the star of four different shows: The Paris Show Car in '66, Earl's Court show London '66, Brussels in '67 and Geneva 1967. I could say it was the star at the LA Auto Show but that wasn't a major show yet. But that got the car to America where the Chinettis, father and son, were Ferrari distributors in New York City.

In September 1967 they sold the car to a New York City Ferrari enthusiast, Marvyn Carton, who bought it for $26,000 trading in his 500 Superfast which the Chinettis only valued at a few thousand (when it was a limited edition worth more than more mass-produced Ferraris) . But the 3-seater was a difficult car to drive in terms of the sunroof and NY summer heat so in March '68 Carton brought it to Chinetti's showroom in

Greenwich CT and sold it back to them.

The next buyer, in '68, was a sometime race car driver named Jan De Vroom, who, incidentally had the best name for a race driver that I ever heard of. (maybe I am partial to the word, having written a Chevrolet ad with the title "Varoom-varoom")

DeVroom, at first glance, seemed to be a high roller. He had a Palm Beach address, and also hung out on the French Riviera. He managed to live the swell life without any apparent income but it was known by many that he was the confidante of an American woman with the imposing title "Marquesa." The woman, Margaret Strong, had married the Spanish Royal who gave her that title. But she was well known before that , by virtue of being a grandaughter of John D. Rockefeller. When he died, she had inherited millions. Her first husband was the ballet-mad Marquis de Cuevas. After he decamped, she had a number of effete men in her retinue, including DeVroom who invested in backing the Chinetti racing team, called NART for North American Racing Team. He bought in with George Arents, another racer, rumored to be his lover. They weren't just investors, they both were accomplished racers and competed in international events.

As a partner in the team, De Vroom didn't have to pay that much for the three seater, as he got $12,000 for trading in his 275 GTB/4, s/n 10827, and thus only paid $6,052 in cash. It was a good buy because the Tre Posti really set him apart from the other rich swells toodling along the Croissette in Cannes in the summer of '68.

A SAD END FOR DE VROOM

I wish I could say De Vroom lived happily ever after.

But it was not to be.

He more or less did himself in by hanging out with the wrong crowd. According to a Vanity Fair article on Margaret, he was alcoholic and a pill popper. And made a practice of inviting drug hustlers to his apartment at all hours. In 1973, two hustlers that he knew rang the bell of his New York apartment. They had successfully hit up De Vroom previously for a $2000 loan. But this time they took a more direct approach-- sending a gangster to demand money and De Vroom protested and was murdered. He was found with his throat cut and number of stab wounds. Adroit PR work kept the name of Margaret de Cuevas out of it and his body was later shipped to Holland. According to the VF article, the killers were caught and tried and, inexplicably, received brief sentences. Vanity Fair's writer even said "It is said that one of them still frequents the bars in New York. "

I have been unable to find if he still owned the three seater when he died but at any rate, in late 1968, it went back to Chinetti and 29 years later the surviving Chinetti. Lou Jr., (nicknamed "Coco") decided to start showing it, entering it in the Meadow Brook Concours in Detroit and the Louis Vuitton Concours in NYC. Three years later it went to two important concours in Europe, the Goodwood Revival in England and the Louis Vuitton in France, and in '01 it went to the Brands Hatch Ferrari festival in the UK.

Thirteen years later he bought it to Gooding & Co's Pebble Beach auction where the high bid was $22,250,000 but failed to win the nod allowing it to be sold from its consignor. It was a no-sale. But, no doubt, it will reappear at another auction and each year, becomes more famous.

Lesson learned? This car, when first seen at auto shows, was salable in the U.S. That was before a car had to meet DOT and NHTSA standards for a production car. Americans, used to automakers not selling prototypes, probably didn't realize, if you bellied up to the bar at a major European show, checkbook in hand, you could buy that car right off the stand.

Now admittedly, it was not tuned to be a race car so would be no good there, and showing of Ferraris in concours hadn't really gotten big at that point, not like today where billionaires vie with each other to have the most storied Ferrari at events like the Pebble Beach concours. So there wasn't much you coud do with it besides drive it on the street, and that blasted sunroof probably boiled the occupants in any warm climate.

But no matter, it was a good rolling conversation piece. So the right time to buy it was when nobody wanted it. Or when Jan De Vroom had enjoyed it for the summer and didn't need it anymore. So note, dear student, in devising your Barn Find Strategies, that cars owned by playboys aren't kept long; they tend to tire of their cars quickly, just like their women.

And that styling of the Tre Posti? Well, sometimes wallflowers grow into swans... something like that.

Chapter 3
The Whatsis Porsche
(1966 The Porsche 911R)
You see a lot of strange things in
West Hollywood...

It is the place where young actors come, hoping to get discovered. They'll do anything to get attention, like own some outlandish car. One day, around 1970, I was walking near Sunset Strip when I spotted a guy leaning on a white Porsche 911. Now, I knew 911 cars. I knew they had horizontal taillights but this one had two circular ones on each side. And it said "911R" on the trunk lid.

The owner introduced himself as Jeff Mannix, and told me he was, of course, an actor. When I said, "I know 911 models, but I never heard of this one," he said it was a special lightweight one, and so light in fact it would lift the front wheels if

he accelerated hard. That was pretty hard to believe, but I asked him if it was for sale. He said it was, and he wanted $7000. Though I had that in the bank, I was skeptical. I hadn't heard of a 911R, so, ergo, it didn't exist, right? I went back to work at Motor Trend, where I was associate editor, and said I'd like to get pictures of this car and do a story.

So we did.

Now flash forward to today—45 years later. I hear 911R Porsches are worth a million dollars.

Each.

So it seems I should look into them more. Mr. Mannix, it turns out, was not misrepresenting the car. While dreamed up by Porsche to run as a GT sports car, they didn't make near enough of them to qualify for homologation, so if you bought one you had to run it against faster, lighter prototypes.

Porsche saw some limited success with them, as private owners ran them in select events in 1967 and 1968.

According to the Revs Institute, a museum-based automotive history organization, the car was pretty much plastic:

> *Except for its steel unibody," they wrote, "the 911R body shell, built by Karl Baur, is 100% fiberglass. So thorough were Porsche's weight-saving measures that the cars were even fitted with special oil tanks in front of the right rear wheel, ultralight taillight assemblies and front turn signals, and, to paint the lily, epoxy plastic door handles unique to these cars which saved possibly a pound. With weight under control, Piëch (a top official of Porsche–Ed.) specified the potent Carrera 6 powerplant. Wide (for the time) alloy wheels were fitted at all four quarters.*
>
> *Porsche attempted to homologate the new car as a 911S variant, but with 50 more hp and at least 350 less pounds, the FIA wasn't buying the story. Market research indicated that selling the 500 units now necessary for homologation couldn't be done profitably, so the 23 911Rs thus far built*

(including three prototypes) were destined to finish their competition careers in non-production categories or as rally cars where homologation wasn't necessary.

The car's one big victory was in the Tour de France relaunch in 1969. Just one car was sent from the factory to France, and Frenchman Gerard Larousse was hired to drive it. How did he beat such big-investment cars as the Ford GT40? Well, the Tour de France is a number of events strung together, and the 911R did well in the hillclimb portion. That and its capability on the roadrace courses put it first overall.

Even though the 911R was not mass produced, Porsche took lessons they learned from it and applied them to the production 911 2.0 T/R, cars customers would be racing in the GT class. 911R production ceased in 1968, and experts now agree that four prototypes and 20 customer cars were made. A website called Total 911 says, "The Porsche 911R was Zuffenhausen's first attempt at a homologation special. However, weighing just 800kg and featuring the Carrera GTS's 210 bhp flat six, the FIA weren't convinced that this was just a variant of a 911S, instead making it race as a prototype." In other words, they tried Ferrari's trick of making just a few and saying it was but a minor variation of an existing already homologated model. But where Ferrari snuck in the 250GTO with that bogus story in '62, by the time Porsche showed up with the 911R, the FIA (which makes the rules) wasn't as easily fooled.

When I brought up my original sighting of the car on a Porsche forum in 2013, a forum poster wrote:

We used to run around up on Mulholland Drive, especially in summer time when you could hang out till 2-3 a.m. This was in 1970-75. One night we hear this tremendous wail echoing off the mountain/canyon walls. Two headlamps were moving FAST coming up the hill from Laurel Canyon. In a flash, I recognized the same R blasting past us. After a collective 'Whoa.....' from the crowd, we *all giggled with glee on how b****in this car sounded and hauled A** past. A few weeks later I cruise into Bob Smith Porsche near Hollywood Boulevard. There on the service drive, niched in the corner, was the R! Holy S! I approach the service manager and ask about the car. 'Its for sale. It's an old 911R, super light, and loud" My heart skipped... "H.h..howwww much?' 'We are asking $8000 bucks' came the answer. Oh my... How am I going to swing this?? Here was the Auto Expo car in front of my face, the Mulholland midnite terror, and it was for sale!!*

That evening the subject was gingerly brought up at the dinner table with Mom and Dad. The subject matter was dropped quickly after being informed that Dad could buy a brand new Cadillac Brougham for slightly less money. But Daad! This is a super rare car! This car is soooo awesome! Subject closed.

A few weeks later my friend Simon, who had rescued a neat lowered '67 SWB from a wrecking yard, told me about these guys with a trick Porsche shop in West Hollywood (where San Vicente and La Cienega cross today) Cool...let's go check it out. Wow! There was the R again, with its rear end propped way up on jack stands and three guys taking the engine out

Dang... Met Jeff Mannix and we chatted a little. The real asking price for the car was SIX THOUSAND ($6,000) DOLLARS. I admired the neat features again one more time—as this was just a dream not to be realized back then.

So, thank you, God, for the Internet. We can now, by dancing our fingers on the keys, find out what happened to cars we viewed once for five minutes almost half a century ago. Read it and weep!

But there's a lesson to be learned here: Don't EVER be big, so damn big, in your britches that, when you come across a car you never heard of before, you are skeptical and think you are being conned.

Mr. Mannix was entirely correct in his representation those many years ago. What he had was a very, very rare car. One so rare it wasn't mentioned in any of the car magazines I read. A car which, had I believed him, I could have enjoyed for the next 44 years and sold today for a million dollars (odds are, though, I would have sold it within a couple years). So, I say be open-minded when you find something unknown. Take notes, take pictures, and follow it up ASAP.

Chapter 4
A Wolf in Wolf's Clothing
(1964 Ferrari 250LM)

Boy, if there was ever a time to get a deal on a LeMans racer, it was when this 250LM was bodied as a Porsche...

This is the story of a world class Ferrari race car that, for a few brief years, ran in mufti; in disguise, not to fool anybody mind you, but because of the plain and simple fact that a Porsche

body was cheaper than a Ferrari body.

First, the car: a 1964 250LM. Ferrari had been successful with front engine sports cars, but around 1960 a revolution happened in racing and a lot of cars started to go mid-engine. Enzo Ferrari dragged his heels in building a mid-engine GT car, but finally built the 250LM, which some joked was merely the 250P race car "with a roof."

Although it didn't win a single race in its introductory year, it showed Ferrari could fight off the Ford GT40, also a mid-engine race car.

There was an epic behind-the-scenes battle with the FIA, the group that sanctions race cars, over whether the 250LM could be homologated as a production car. The FIA required 100 examples of a car be built for it to be homologated, and Ferrari originally sought to fool them the same way he did with the 250GTO two years earlier. But the FIA counted the LMs and found less than 40, so it was forced to run in the prototype class.

But Ferrari got his revenge when one of his distributor's

cars—that of the Chinetti team from North America—actually won the 24 hours of LeMans in '65 when the Ford team GT40s broke one by one.

Enzo Ferrari probably derived particular enjoyment that the winning car was driven by Jochen Rindt and American Masten Gregory, who had been left off the Ford GT team.

This particular car, Chassis Number 5899 GT, was the ninth 250LM made, completed by the factory on June 3, 1964. Like most 250LMs, it was painted *Rossa Cina* and upholstered with Panno Blu seats. Six weeks later, it was shipped off to Count Filipinetti's scuderia in Switzerland.

Now, it turns out that, going back to 1955, Switzerland had outlawed car racing, horrified, as everyone was, by the big crash at LeMans where a Mercedes went into the crowd, killing over 80 people. But they did allow hillclimbs. Filipinetti's first outing with the 250LM was the Sierre-Montana Crans Hill Climb on August 30, 1964. The car was driven by Ludovico Scarfiotti, one of Ferrari's top Formula One drivers and a man who happened to be the winner of the 1963 24 Hours of Le Mans. He took 1st overall. And then repeated the victory at the XV Coppa Intereuropa at Monza.

But my favorite driver in that era was a Sicilian schoolteacher who doubled as a race driver—Nino Vaccarella, also a Ferrari Formula One driver and the winner of the 1964 24 Hours of Le Mans. He also drove the Fillipinetti LM to victory.

But the string of victories was short lived, because, at the 1000Km of Paris, Vaccarella and Jean Guichet had to drop out after an accident damaged the radiator. That was the car's last race for the Swiss team.

NEW TEAM, NEW HOPE

But the car did not leave Switzerland right away. In '65, it was sold off the stand at that year's Geneva Motor Show to architect Werner Biedermann, of Zürich. He ran it under the banner of Ecurie Basilisk, of Basel, Switzerland. The car did well at fifteen events.

But Switzerland being an extremely mountainous place, the laws of gravity are always threatening and, with Biedermann behind the wheel, the car slid off the road and flipped onto its roof during a practice run up the mountain for the SAR Engelberg Hill Climb. Biedermann stepped out of the upside-down car unhurt, but later sold the car to Hans Illert, of Feldmeilen, Switzerland.

A SHEEP-KILLER IN WOLF'S CLOTHING

Here is where the car went into disguise, as it were. Illert wanted to get the car back out on the track, but Switzerland does not have the panel beaters Italy does. So he did the next best thing—when he heard a mid-engine Porsche (aka 905) body was available, he bought it and shortened the Ferrari chassis to carry the fiberglass body.

He also tried to make it look sorta Ferrari-ish, but the gull-wing doors revealed the body's source. At least you could say the good part about this conversion was that the car was 200 Kg lighter. Illert re-dubbed it the "LM-P."

The car was campaigned by Scuderia Tartaruga, and driven by Illert at the 23rd annual St. Ursanne-Les Rangiers Hill Climb in Switzerland on August 20 and 21, 1966, where he showed he had prepped it right because he finished 1st. The car became a stalwart of motorsports events in Switzerland during the 1966 season.

The following year, the first big event was a slalom at the Dübendorf Airfield, where Illert's LM-P placed first in class. That whole '67 season was fought hard with good results, as Swiss drivers Dieter Spörry, and Heini Walter joined Illert behind the wheel.

Illert sold the car in early 1968 to another Swiss, Pierre Sudan, of Zug. Sudan wanted more power, so he took out the car's original 3.3-liter engine and replaced it with a 4.0-liter unit from a 330 P (stamped Number 0818), which he bought from British privateer David Piper. Sudan began referring to the car as the "330 LM-P," to properly identify its new powertrain.

He competed in hillclimbs through '68, running in events as

far away as Belgium.

As the season ended, Sudan ran an ad in *Auto Motor und Sport* to sell his car. The next owner was an Austrian shop, Autoreparatur Handelsverwertungs GmbH.

The car was actively campaigned by Stefan Sklenar in hillclimbs and other German and Austrian events, including the 200 Miles of Nürnberg and the Tyrolean Grand Prix, in the summer of 1969.

CRASH #2

But the car went off the road again in 1970, leaving the Porsche body unrepairable.

Various entrepreneurs bought it in turn, first Paul Blancpain and then Swiss writer and historian Rob de la Rive Box, but they couldn't get traction on finding a new 250LM-like body.

That didn't happen until a well known Ferrari enthusiast, Paul Schouwenburg, entered the picture. Schouwenburg is a famous cancer surgeon who has barn-found several rare Alfas, including a 1900CSS Zagato and Tipo 33/2, and dozens of very special Ferraris, including a 250GTO, 340 America Touring, 250 MM Vignale Berlinetta, 250GT SWB Competition/61, and a 275GTB/C/LM. When he found them and bought them, he would usually hop in, gas up, and drive home—no matter where the starting point was. His book, *Ferrari Fever*, tells all the stories, and is a must-read for everybody who dreams about stumbling onto bits of automotive history. Anyway, Schouwenburg bought the car. One of the first things he did to get the car back to original was to buy back the car's original 3.3-liter—through David Piper, who took back what was originally his 4.0-liter V-12 in trade.

REVIVAL OF CHASSIS NO. 5899 GT

But Schouwenberg got an offer from a music-world icon. Eric Stewart, of the British pop band 10cc, who saw the car's potential and bought it. In 1977, he retained Victor Norman and Bob Houghton of England's Rosso Limited in Cirencester to make a new body in alloy. The original chassis was sent first to Ferrari's Assistenza Clienti in Modena and then to William Vaccari for restoration. The restored car arrived back in the UK in May, 1981, when Stewart put on his driving suit, helmet, and gloves and seated himself for a few laps around Goodwood, a famous track owned by a British Lord that is now the site of some famous historic events. Then he sold it to Peter Grohof Trefenbronn, Germany, for $160,000.

It next changed hands, for $190,000, to a San Diego shop that imported exotic cars. In the tonier LaJolla part of town was famed collector Said Marouf, who bought it, kept it for some years, then sold it to a buyer in Japan. It left Japan in 1992 for Europe, and returned to England when Lord Irvine Laidlaw, a very significant collector and model practitioner of The Good Life, caught wind of the car and bought it in July, 1995. "Sir Sex Addict", as The Daily Mail later called him, then had it fully overhauled and serviced by Phil Stainton.

Now, you would think the restorations done to this point would be enough. But no, each Ferrari collector has his own way of seeing how a car should be done, so when Lord Laidlaw sold it two years later to Federico Della Noce and Andrè Lara Resende, they commissioned the car's third restoration, which was done at Dino Cognolato's Carrozzeria Nova Rinascente in Vigonza, Italy. The mechanical parts were done at Corrado Patella. Final preparation was done at Carrozzeria Autosport di Bacchelli e Villa in Bastiglia where, of course, the original shade of red paint was laid on.

At some point, the car got a new chassis to replace the original, which had first been altered to fit the Porsche body in 1966, then was re-altered to fit the Rosso Limited alloy body commissioned by Eric Stewart in 1977.

The Della Noce and Resende restoration was done in time for the car to appear on track at the Shell Historic Ferrari Maserati Challenge in October, 2000. For five years, Della Noce and Resende ran the car at events around the world at venues including Laguna Seca, Monza, and Brands Hatch.

FERRARI'S BLESSING

The most important thing that can happen to a Ferrari these days is to get the Classiche certification by the factory, equivalent to the Pope absolving you of all your sins. On April 13, 2005, the car's provenance was certified by Ferrari, a process described thusly by auction house RM's catalog for a 2015 auction of the car: "Chassis 5899 GT was granted Classiche certification by the factory, with its vaunted Red Book confirming the quality and authenticity of its restoration and repairs."

In 2006, Della Noce and Resende sold the car to another Swiss collector, Henri-Louis Maunoir.

In a weird coincidence, Maunoir is married to Georges Filipinetti's granddaughter, Samantha, bringing the car around full circle to the first family that owned it. Maunoir showed it at Ferrari's 60th anniversary festivities at Fiorano in 2007, and at the 60th anniversary of Ecurie Francorchamps in Spa-Francorchamps, Belgium, in May, 2012.

When offered at auction by RM, they pointed out that the car came compete with "a meticulously detailed Massini report that documents ownership from new." Marcel Massini is a Swiss national who is hired by clients around the world to come by and investigate the authenticity of their Ferraris. His archive of photos alone includes 25,000 pictures. And, of course, since you spend millions on such a vetting, you also get the original owner's manual in a leather pouch, and a proper tool roll.

On Friday, January 16, 2015, RM sold the car at auction for $9,625,000. Lesson to be learned? I have no doubt that this car was passed up by many who frowned at the idea of a Ferrari with a Porsche body. Some probably thought, with the frame shortened, who would know how to properly lengthen it to fit a proper LM body? Ironically, it was while being raced as a Porsche/Ferrari mismatch that this particular 250LM represented the most interesting of barn-find possibilities. It was a diamond masquerading as a rhinestone to be sure.

Chapter 5
Too Slow on the Draw, Pahdnuh
(1964 Pininfarina Mercedes 230SL)
On why you have to move fast...

Around '70 to '72, I was working as an associate editor at *Motor Trend* magazine on Sunset Strip. Right across the street from our building was a dealer who sold exotic cars. About once a week, from my perch six floors up, I would see an extraordinary car pop into the lot. The car's owner would try to sell it to the dealer and then, invariably disappointed at the offer, the car owner would leave.

One week, as I peered down from my aerie, I saw the car was a Mercedes 230SL coupe. A fixed head coupe. I knew it was special, since those cars normally came with lift-off hardtops. But I was on the sixth floor and told myself it was no use running down six flights of stairs.

It would have taken too long to get down to the street to find out who owned it and what they wanted for it.

So I bumbled on through life, occasionally reading about the

car I missed, the fabled Pininfarina 230SL coupe.

According to Tom Tjaarda (pronounced Jur-DUH), an American who was from Michigan like me but went to Italy in 1959 to design cars and never came back, the idea for the car first came from Pininfarina, which hoped to get a contract from Mercedes to make more than one. Pininfarina had done some earlier work for Mercedes, but never succeeded in getting a production contract for a series.

Mercedes looked at Pininfarina's proposal with a jaundiced eye. After all, their car had only just been unveiled and here they were, two months later, getting a letter from Pininfarina (to Karl Wilfert) asking to be allowed to modify a 230SL (and presumably asking for a chassis to be donated).

The Board approved and Tjaarda had free rein, changing as much of the car as he could to give it an Italian flair.

For instance, the pagoda lift-off roof was done away with and it became a fixed head coupe. He kept the grille and head-lamps of the original, but he raked the grille back more sharply, edged a sculptural flare to the fenders and flared out the sides. The rear was reminiscent of his earlier Ferrari production car, the 330GT 2+2, but still totally 230SL. Inside, to save money, the dashboard was unchanged but the stitching on the interior oozed Italian hand craftsmanship.

The bubble headlamps, available on European Mercedes models, were much more modern looking than the circular sealed-beam lamps used in the States—plus you could use the "running light" function in Euro cities at night, so as not to glare at pedestrians. I like the grille in the stock 230SL better; to me, it looks stronger than the Pininfarina treatment.

The side view is more graceful than typical Mercedes lift-off hardtops, mindful of other Tjaarda designs at the time. He favored light and airy greenhouses. A sharpened crease running the full length of car over the upper parts of the fenders adds boldness and strength to the car, like the crease in a well-tailored suit. The stock hubcaps make it look budget-oriented; too bad there wasn't enough money in the program to do Tjaarda's own wheel designs, as he did on many other cars.

The rear view was pleasing, its downturned trunklid more modern than what Mercedes chose for their mass production car. Taillights look added on, like "what can we find in a parts bin that will fit into this space," but are still better than stock 230SL taillights which are way overladen, in typical Germanic fashion, with fat chrome surrounds.

Alas, no new interior was designed. No doubt the decision to keep the stock interior was budget driven, but it looks very old fashioned when set into the more modern exterior. I like the carpeted, ribbed rear ledge behind the seats, very oh-so-Continental. Where's the fitted luggage?

Overall, it is an interesting take on the 230SL design, one with much more of an overall matched front-to-rear design than the one from Mercedes' drawing boards. Still, we will never know if there would have been a market for it.

Other features were wrap-around bumpers, a more elongated tapering nose, and Tjaarda's "trademark," a tall, airy "greenhouse."

The car had several owners between the time I first saw it and the time it reached the late Weston Hook of La Jolla, California. At the Turin show, at least 30 people purportedly wanted to buy it, but publisher Axel Springer was triumphant and he later gave it to his ex-wife, Rosemarie.

There was another owner in Monaco (where better to have a one-off car?) and then it came to America, to Palm Springs, where it was bought by Joe Morell. It was he who changed it from its original light color to black (including putting on stock wheels and painting the center caps black), and he who then painted it red.

When Weston Hook saw it in 1997 and bought it, he had the idea of returning it to its original 1964 configuration. He chose restorer Jerry Hjeltness from Escondido to do that, and the result won first place in the European sports car class at the 1997 Pebble Beach Concours d'Elegance. The odd coincidence was that the voting jury included not only former Pininfarina designer Tom Tjaarda, but also Bruno Sacco, at the time still Mercedes-Benz Design Chief. (Ah, but to be a fly on the wall and hear Sacco's comments, for basically the car was designed as an alternative to his production design).

Lesson learned? I was too lazy to run down six flights or stairs. But I could have at least asked around of local Mercedes mechanics; one might have told me who owned it. Or I could have joined the Mercedes club and looked at the roster. But the car went out of my mind soon after I saw it, and it was only decades later that I realized it was, by virtue of being a one-off car by an esteemed Italian coachbuilder, a million-dollar car.

Chapter 6
A Caddy Named Jackie
(1960 Cadillac Pininfarina)
Wherein a shell becomes a running prototype...

Politics aside, you gotta admit that, back in the day, Jackie Kennedy was a trend setter. As wife of the President, what she wore was mentioned in all the fashion columns. So it was that a European design  firm built a prototype and named it after her, maybe hoping she would pose by it and they might all get some headlines. That never happened. Oh, they built the car, but you don't easily wrangle the wife of the President into pimping your car-design proposal for you.

The design firm was Pinin Farina—then in the process of changing its name to Pininfarina.

Cadillac and Pininfarina had long-standing ties. Back in 1959, Pininfarina did some production Cadillac Broughams and later on, decades after this prototype, Cadillac came to Pininfarina for the ill-fated Allante.

Very obscure (especially what happened to them) were a couple of styling exercises Pinin Farina did on Cadillacs: the Starlight Coupe and Starlight convertible for the '58 and '60 Paris salons.

But in October, 1960, came a more modern looking Cadillac-based show car, one sans tailfins, called the Jacqueline. Pininfarina might have been hoping it would kickstart a new bodied-in-Italy program at GM. If that was their hope, it died a-bornin'.

When first unveiled, the Jaqueline was painted in Ermine White, a Cadillac color. The design was clean and simple, maybe too simple considering the Cadillacs made in Michigan were competing with Chrysler over who could build the tallest tailfin.

On this one, the tail sloped downward, but the highlight of the car was the large glass area and stainless steel roof that enclosed the passenger compartment.

Really cheeky was the idea that it was a two-seater, Europeans found it incredibly wasteful that a car this long—130" wheelbase—only had seating for two. Pininfarina should have known this would diminish GM's interest from the get-go, as the only two-seater they had in production at the time was the Corvette. And GM was still losing money on every Corvette sold.

Now, one reason you didn't see the car driving around was that it was a "pushmobile," industry jargon for an auto-show concept car with no engine or drivetrain. It had four wheels mounted to a tube frame. Pinin Farina was selling designs, not drivetrains.

Pininfarina was undiminished in their zeal to get a GM contract, going on from the Jackie to build the Corvette Rondine, the Corvair Pininfarina Coupe Speciale, and others, but never succeeded in getting a contract for a production car until the Allante, which only came about when GM came to them hat in hand.

Once it was designated as the design that had failed to cause heart flutter in Detroit, the Jacqueline went into Pininfarina's own museum in Turin.

THE BIG SLEEP

There it went into "Big Sleep" mode and sat for 30 years.

Now, contrary to American companies, who like to crush concept cars lest they fall into the hands of future litigants, Italian coachbuilders sometimes sells prototypes, even non-running ones. They sold this one sometime in the mid-1990s to a Belgian Ferrari dealer named Philippe Lancksweert, who later sold it to Michel Kruch of Brussels in partnership with another collector, Herve Irving Willems. During all this changing of hands, it was repainted gold.

If you want to show up at a toney concours like Pebble Beach, it helps if the car is running. So when Alain-Dominique Perrin, then CEO of the French Cartier group, bought the car, he sent it to a shop in Florida, Harbor Auto Restorations, with instructions to make it a running car.

The irony is that, when originally built, the only Cadillac content was the Cadillac badge—and even that Pininfarina had modified.

Harbor bought a 1960 Cadillac Eldorado Biarritz so they could put under the body the engine and chassis the Jacqueline never had.

The donor chassis was fitted with a 1959 vintage Series 62 V-8 that displaced 390 cubic inches and was rated at 325 horsepower. The suspension was comprised of front coil springs, rear leaf springs, and hydraulic shock absorbers on all four corners. It was given a working steering system, essential gauges and instrumentation, operating foot pedals, and the appropriate wiring.

Turning a pushmobile into a running car is no easy task. Think about it: you have to add a fuel system, electricals, an engine, a transmission, a cooling system; the whole nine yards. Not to mention all the glass in the original show car was plexiglass, so you had to get new glass made all around. But as a finished car it was a success at the Bagatelle Concours d'Elegance in Paris in 1998 and 2000, and impressed Americans new to the car at the 1999 Concorso Italiano.

It was brought to the 2007 Monterey Sports & Classic Car Auction presented by RM Auctions, where they estimated its value at $350,000 to $450,000. Bidding reached $260,000 but it was not enough to clear the reserve. Considering what it cost to make a running car, I can see why the seller had a high reserve.

The car reportedly changed hands again, and this writer is unaware of its current location.

Lesson learned? You could've bought this car a lot cheaper before it came to America. Most people, even fans of European coachbuilders, never think, "Hey, I wonder what they still got in the barn?"

Still, this car falls into a class that I have quandaries about. Can a body with a "chassis" that is only designed to work to hold up the body but not one intended for a running driving car be considered a car at all or just a piece of rolling sculpture? Yet other auto show concept cars, such as the Ferrari Pinin, also a pushmobile, were eventually made running cars (though at least that had been built with an engine). On the other hand, the price bid at auctions shows there is some interest in such cars even as sculptures, even if they are not ever fully operable road cars (add another $200,000 if you want that).

So, if you visit a coachbuilder's museum, schmooze them a little, ask to look at the basement, the back room, hell, even out in the back 40 (when I visited Pininfarina I saw a one-off Ferrari 308GTB more or less in the junk pile). You never know what you're gonna find…

Chapter 7
A Present from Uncle Adolph
(1939 Mercedes 540K Cabriolet C)
Hey, to Hitler it was like handing out candy bars...

Adolf Hitler was getting ready to start WWII, and figured a smart move would be making nice with various rulers of areas with oil.

One such leader, a wet-behind-the-ears king of Egypt named Farouk, was getting married, and Hitler thought a Mercedes 540K cabriolet would make a nice present–and serve as a good sales promotion for The Third Reich.

Somebody once said of the car, "If Thor, the god of Thunder, owned a car it would be a Supercharged Mercedes."

True then, and true now.

Surprisingly, Mercedes had already put a supercharger on a car in 1919. Racing archives show many models that won with a puffer, from the 1922 Targa Florio winner to the W125 and W154 Grand Prix cars just before the second world war, not to mention supercharged street cars like the SSK and SSKL. Before ceasing production of road cars to make military vehicles, the 500K and 540K werethe last supercharged production models. The 500K came along in 1934 to replace the 380. Fortunately, Germany also got autobahns at the time, and one could cruise at 80 mph.

"K" is for "King"

The King's car was a 500K Cabriolet B, powered by a 5,019 cc straight eight making 160b.h.p. with the supercharger engaged or 100 without.

The noise the car made when one's foot was deep into it was, according to H.S. Linfield of The Autocar in 1936, "an almost demoniacal howl."

The car also had a sophisticated chassis. Its helical-spindle steering was an evolved version of the preceding 380's. Front suspension used new double-wishbone axles with coil springs. In the rear were double-jointed swing axles with double-coil springs and an additional transverse balancing spring. A vacuum-boosted service brake acted hydraulically on all four wheels. It was heavy. Very heavy. The chassis alone weighed as much as 1,700 kilograms; the complete car over 2,300 kilograms.

Most customers accepted the coachwork from the factory, but there were those who went to outside coachbuilders in Sindelfingen. Over a two-year period, 342 500Ks were cranked out. Then, when the more powerful 540K came along, a lot of owners switched over to that car and its supercharged 180 hp. engine. Most experts believe 319 were made. It would cruise at 100 mph. The long-wheelbase variant, the so-called "normal" chassis with the radiator directly above the front axle, was the backbone for the four-seat cabriolet B (with four side windows) and the elegant C (with two side windows) and, at a later stage, also for touring cars and saloons.

The King's car, chassis no. 169387, made its debut at the 1936 Internationale Automobilausstellung in Berlin. The car was subsequently bought by the German government—the Fuhrer needing just the right present for King Farouk I on his wedding day, January 20, 1938. Not that the King needed it; he had over 100 cars already.

THIS COLOR RESERVED FOR ROYALTY

On Farouk's orders, the car was repainted the royal Egyptian color of dark red.

A decree was then issued outlawing all red cars in Egypt. If you saw one, you knew straightaway a Royal was coming.

Not that the King enjoy it for too long. In '52, he was forced out and the poor guy spent the rest of his life in Paris, Italy, and on the Cote d'Azur—the latter location leading to tales of wretched excess involving drink, gambling and women.

Somehow, the specter of it being a Royal car was so strong that nobody thought of selling it until 1988, when 169387 was bought at auction and stored in a French barn by a French collector. Flash forward 18 years: in 1996 a Mercedes restorer was asked to inspect the car. It was then brought it back to Germany and restored, a process that took five years. It was auctioned in Monaco on May 20, 2006, and sold for just over 92,000 Euros, which seems a bargain indeed.

Lesson learned? Rulers come. Rulers go. Sometimes it takes a helluva long time after they're gone before anyone works up the nerve to see what was left behind. Though Nasser, who succeeded Farouk, ordered Farouk's treasures sold in 1954, somehow this car escaped the net until 1966. Whoever got it then no doubt got a bargain. So the lesson is that, even long after a ruler or despot (sometimes they are one and the same) leaves the head job, their toys might still be around. It behooves you to make inquiries...

Chapter 8
Dream Car for Sale
(1976 Ferrari 308GT4)
Some say I was always chasing Rainbows...

Way back, when I was a younger lad, I cheekily wrote Carrozzeria Bertone and asked if they wanted to sell the Rainbow concept car.

They actually replied, and said they would for $250,000. Or I could have a replica built.

I demurred.

Bertone had done my favorite Ferrari, the one-off, split-grille 250GT SWB designed by Giugiaro. The 308GT4 was a wedge, like the 308GT4 production car they were building for Ferrari but more extreme in every way. I really wasn't crazy about it, I just wanted something "one off." (one off the assembly line)

The Rainbow was a great leap into the future from the Dino 308GT4, which Bertone had already been building for Ferrari. The Rainbow had an unusual top that could be flipped back behind the seats to make an open car.

The chassis was shortened by 10 cm, and I can now say it wouldn't have fit me at 6'1", since my Ferrari 308GTS by their rival Pininfarina was a tight fit.

The Rainbow made its debut at the 1976 Turin Motor Show, and made a good impression because of its unique top design. You might say it's a retractable hardtop, but it was not automatic—it required manual effort to remove, fold, and stow in the back. The design is attributed to designer Marcello Gandini and, to tell the truth, methinks he was pushing beyond where Ferrari wanted to go. Too much wedge, I'd say.

The public wasn't used to flat planes and wedge shapes at that time, but after the Gandini-designed Lamborghini Countach and Ferrari 308GT4 (on which the Rainbow was built) became commonplace, the public finally understood the Rainbow. Almost unacceptable was the odd rear wheel well tire cutout coming down at about 45 degrees over the wheelwell. We could take the extreme wedge, but we wanted our wheelwells following the shape of our wheels.

An unattributed article in *CAVALLINO* implied that Bertone was miffed he didn't get the two-seater coupe contract from Ferrari (it went to Pininfarina), so he built the Rainbow in revenge.

The car with headlights down was decent but, when the headlights were up, the front aspect was horrible, like the Fiat X1/9. Not to mention the taillights weren't round; maybe he didn't want to look like he was copying Pininfarina. It was a very "color sensitive" design; i.e. it looked far better in silver than in ice-box white.

Gandini also redid the dashboard, so it's now one long slab with black-rimmed gauges jammed into it similar to the Giugiaro-designed '60s Ghibli. On the right are odd perforations; maybe covering a radio speaker?

One other comment on its design—it uses unusual wheels that have a straight cross section about 6" wide that is very un-Ferrari like. When ol' Nuccio pushed the envelope, he went whole hog!

The Rainbow sat in Bertone's private museum collection, having narrowly avoided joining the leftover concepts that went to the RM Auctions Villa d'Este sale in March, 2011, where six were sold to private collectors.

After having ceased trading because of financial difficulties, Bertone on March 18, 2014, confirmed that it would be declaring bankruptcy. Even though it escaped the fate of the earlier batch of show cars sold in 2014, by 2015 the banks were anxious to recover some of the investment so the remaining 79 prototypes went on sale including the Rainbow. The deal was cockamamie because the "problem" of this auction was an Italian decree about this collection of cars: they must not leave Italy and they cannot be divided for individual sales. In the end, after 40 bids, the whole Bertone collection was sold to ASI for almost 3.5 million Euros. ASI is the Italian Historic Car and Bikes Club; the association which federates all the Italian clubs so it's obvious that all the cars will end up in a museum. But as anyone who is reading this series knows, museums sell cars too, so don't give up. So, am I mad I couldn't buy 12788? Not really. At the end of the day, I decided I still like curves instead of flat planes. No offense, Marcello.

Chapter 9
The Postman's GTO
(1963 Ferrari 250GTO)

Hey, your occupation might not matter if you're first in line with the cash...

What if you were a postman and somebody offered you a tatty old race car? You would think, well, that could be expensive to repair, but what the hell...you only live once, right?

That's the story of a Frenchman named Lenglet, who bought a Ferrari GTO right before they hit it big with collectors.

First, a little bit about the GTO. "Aerodynamics are for people who can't build engines," Enzo Ferrari is said to have said. Compare a 250GT SWB in profile with a Jaguar E-type. The E-type was streets ahead aerodynamically, since Malcolm Sayer, an aircraft designer, was instrumental in its shape. So Enzo assigned engineer Giotto Bizzarrini, then in his employ, to design a more

aerodynamic body for the GTO, one that could beat the E-type.

The GTO's top speed is probably over 170mph. And, it turned out, Enzo worried needlessly; the E-type wasn't that reliable in racing.

The 250GTO was one of the last racing Ferraris that could still be driven on the road. It is very rare; only 36 copies exist, and almost each one of them has a dramatic history.

HOW THE GOAT CAME TO BE

The car came about when, for the 1962 Manufacturer's Championship, the factory's attention switched from sports prototypes to GT cars. Ferrari built the 250 Gran Turismo Omologato (GTO), the last word meaning "homologated," because Ferrari intended to slide it by as a mere variation of the existing short-wheelbase 250GT, bypassing the need to make 100 of them, normally the rule for getting a car homologated in the GT class.

Since Ferrari had already built nearly 200 competition cars based on the 250GT, the FIA approved the GTO homologation. The FIA would soon regret its decision.

Bizzarrini was given his own small team to develop the car, and dispensed with stylists. What the hell do you need them for? Instead, he took a mule and slapped on a different nose shape each night using the Italian version of Bondo, then ran it on the Autostrada. The design with the fastest point-to-point time earned the car its needle-nose shape. He also moved the V-12 engine rearward and lower than in the 250GT SWB, and installed a 5-speed. It was one of the first Ferrari road cars to have a "Kamm effect" rear end, the name referring to Dr. Wunibald Kamm, a German aerodynamicist who developed the theory that a chopped-off tail had good aero.

No less an expert driver than Stirling Moss was hired to drive a GTO at Monza. Moss like it so much he ordered one for himself, but was never able to collect it after he had a life threatening crash at Goodwood.

THE FIRST GTO

Ferrari had a press conference on February 24, 1962, rolling out the GTO and five other cars. One source says the first GTO was chassis 3223GT.

The key to the GTO's success was not only the shape, but the engine, tweaked over the version Bizzarrini had developed for the 250GT SWB Competitzione. It had larger valves, tighter clearances, lighter materials, and dry sump lubrication. You could run it up to 9500 rpm. Basically, it was an outgrowth of the engine used in the 250 Testa Rossa.

The old 250GT SWB chassis got new front brakes, Koni adjustable shock absorbers, a stiffer suspension, and a lower drive line.

Inside, the driver was not coddled. No heater. No sound-proofing. No speedometer. Well, there was a Nardi wood-rimmed steering wheel, if you want luxury. The Borletti/Veglia tach read to 10,000 rpm and was jammed into a binnacle it shared with smaller diameter temperature, fuel, and oil-pressure gauges.

Other teams tried to protest against the GTO's acceptance as a GT car but, if you read the rules, Appendix J, Section 254, said that any modifications introduced after homologation did not disqualify the car if those modifications were a "normal evolution of the type." Since the GTO was an "evolution" of the largely produced 250GT road car, it was declared legal, although the five-speed gearbox and dry sump lubrication were never factory road-car options. So Ferrari got away with it, laughing all the way to the bank. However, when he came out with the mid-engined 250LM later, the FIM punished him by not approving it as a GT car in its first year.

Our car was first built in 1963 for Pierre Dumany, a Frenchman, but was actually campaigned by Ecurie Francochaps, in Belgium. They "cheated" the car a little by installing a 20-liter oil sump. She ran at Le Mans in '63, finishing fourth overall. The biggest victory in period was in the Tour de France, with Lucien Bianchi and Jojo Berger sharing driving tasks. In '65, she finally got the Ecurie Francochamps all-yellow paint job.

Pierre de Siebenthal sold it to a Spaniard, known only as Delgado, who owned it from 1966-70 and still ran the Italian original license plate, MO 84265.

THE POSTMAN RINGS ONCE

In Spain, the car was then bought by a postman, another Frenchman, Monsieru Lenglet of Romainville. Lenglet got it cheap because it was outmoded, the mid-engined 250LM having recently come out.

The price for the GTO was approximately 2 million pesetas in Barcelona in the year 1970. According to a currency conversion chart, that was $13,475 USD (very comparable to the price I was offered a 250GTO for in 1970 - $14,000).This particular car was parked in a flimsy garage on Rosellon street in Barcelona. But when Lenglet tried to bring it to France, according to CAVALLINO magazine, the French customs people harassed him to no end. "No yellow headlights," they said. So he painted them translucent yellow. "The car is too low," they said. So an embittered Lenglet kept the car in his garage for the next 16 years. Meanwhile, he drove a Simca.

He finally began to worry it would get stolen as it increased in value. He sold it to Mr. Henri Chambonin 1986.

Chambon raced it in the Tour de France, then it went on to other owners and is now one of the elite Ferraris in the world.

When I was writing this book, I made inquiries as to the postman. Fortunately for him, I guess, I didn't find out any more than his last name, because forever more, if he is still with us, he might be reminded again by his car-loving friends of the 250GTO he sold for a song.

Lesson learned? You never know what happens to once prominent cars. It behooves you to start an action file on various cars that float your boat, no matter how far-fetched it seems right now that you will ever get a chance to buy them. That's because those who can afford to buy these cars when they are new often have short attention spans—sometimes they barely learn the shift pattern in the one they have before they are off to the latest, greatest model, leaving the old one in the driveway of the car dealer. This postman was in the right place at the right time. He just didn't have a plan for the long game – one what he would do with it if he couldn't afford it. That's essential, but your first job is to be in that place, check in hand, by dint of your advance work and very thorough research.

And, oh, did I mention that 250GTOs are now worth $50 million? Each?

Chapter 10
The Hoarder's Bug
(1937 Bugatti Type 57S)
Hey, why bother to tell your relatives what's in the barn...

O.K. car fans, you hear these horror stories about hoarders—there's even a reality TV show about them, where weekly you see relatives tussling with their crazy uncle or dad or mother or aunt, a hoarder always buried six feet deep in debris because, damn it, he won't throw anything away.

Imagine, if you will, a family in Gosforth, England, near Newcastle-on-Tyme (yes, the English really do have quaint hyphenated town names like that). This is back in the first decade of the 2000s. Now the basic family members are not hoarders. My definition: they can still see the floor in every room. But there's this one bachelor uncle, a retired medical doctor, living in a separate house on the property. It is rumored he has a few cars stashed away in the family garage, but nobody remembers quite what kind of cars they are.

Dr. Harold Carr, it turns out, was quite the hoarder of old things mechanical. If it was a gizmo, he loved it. An orthopedic surgeon who served as an army doctor during World War II, he was also a keen flier, and, after the war, flew several vintage airplanes. He bought a Bugatti in 1955 for £895 when the Pound Sterling was worth close to $5.

According to Chris Brooke of the *Daily Mail* website in January, 2009, "When eccentric doctor and compulsive hoarder Harold Carr died at the age of 89, his relatives faced a daunting task to sort through his possessions. His home was packed with piles of medical machinery, 1,500 beer steins, thousands of receipts, and even a World War Two spy drone. But all the effort became worth it when they opened the door of his garage—and struck gold."

Four wheeled gold: a 1937 Bugatti.

A nephew said, "We knew he had some cars, but we had no idea what they were. It was a bit of local folklore that he had a Bugatti, but no one knew for sure. It's worth so much because he hasn't used it for 50 years. It was one of the original supercars.

He described his uncle as a very eccentric old gent, adding: "I suppose you could call him a mad doctor. People who saw him in the street thought he was a tramp. He would wear two pairs of trousers at the same time.

"All the children would laugh at him in the street when he tinkered with his cars because he wore a piece of rubber tube round his head to stop the oil getting in his hair. But he was always such a generous man."

Today such a lifestyle would be classified as a form of obsessive-compulsive disorder, where you hoard everything in your house and refuse to leave. The debris, piled six feet high at his detached home, included receipts for things as trivial as pencils he had bought in the 1950s. It took his relatives 18 months to get the house cleaned up enough to sell.

And the Bugatti wasn't the only car in the stash. A classic Aston Martin was found in another garage, and his relatives were able to sell that for "tens of thousands." But the poor E-type Jaguar was so far gone that it had to be scrapped.

Once the Bugatti was unearthed, and its discovery hit the newspapers, offers poured in from all over the world. But even before that, when it was still "secret," his relatives told reporters that notes regularly got pushed through his door mail slot. People traveled from all over the world in attempts to try and convince him to sell the Bugatti (I can only think they knew of it by looking at old Bugatti club newsletters and seeing his name and city of residence.)

What made the find all the more remarkable is that it punched the right buttons in terms of provenance: it was owned by Earl Howe and Lord Ridley, both key figures in Bugatti racing.

And because it was hidden away so long, it reeked of originality, still claiming the original chassis, engine, drivetrain, and body. And here's a kicker—when found, after being buried in debris for over 50 years, the odometer read just 26,284 miles.

ABOUT THE CAR

First, a little about this car's history. Chassis No. 57502 was completed at the Bugatti works on May 5, 1937, sporting two-seat Atalante coupe coachwork.

Two years after Bugatti introduced its 1930s masterpiece, the Type 57, the model evolved into its definitive form as the S or competition model. Compared to the original Type 57s, the 57S had increased performance and a lowered center of gravity created by running the car's rear axle through the chassis.

Chassis No. 57502 was ordered new by the British Racing Drivers' Club's first President, Earl Howe, via the UK Bugatti agents, Sorel of London. Howe had a long association with Ettore Bugatti and his son, Jean, having raced their Grand Prix cars for years.

Earl Howe took delivery in June, 1937, and kept the car for eight years. He only slightly updated it, adding, for instance, his own bumpers, rear-view mirrors on the A-pillars, and a luggage rack, all of which were on the car when unearthed.

During the war, Earl Howe served with the Royal Navy Volunteer Reserve but, since there was gas rationing, there was no racing...

Two years after the war, it was sold through a dealership named Continental Cars to a Mr. J.P. Tingay. It was he who brought the car up to 'SC' specification by fitting a Marshall K200 supercharger. Not an original Bugatti part, true, but one could say it was "a period fitment" (using parts available and installed back when Bugattis were still being made).

A Mr. M.H. Ferguson acquired the Bugatti from Tingay in 1950 and then, four years later, it went to Lord Ridley's collection. Only a year after that, Bugatti enthusiast Dr Harold Carr bought it and used it as a road car. In the early '60s, Dr. Carr put it in his garage, retiring Chassis No. 57502 from the road, so to speak.

THE BIG SLEEP

It then entered that ignominious phase of some collector cars that I call "the big sleep," this time for half a century.

Move the hands of the clock forward to 2007, Dr. Carr dies.

His relatives find the car and somehow it escapes the clutches of a car dealer and goes to an auction company, stopping on the way to get cleaned up a bit. Bear in mind the car was sold unrestored, in adherence to a fast-growing movement in the car-collecting field. "Unrestored" has become a phrase that anoints a car with holiness, because it means all the original parts can be restored or conserved in order to maintain originality.

RARITY MAKES IT A WINNER

Rarity counts a lot in a car's value. Bugatti historians say six racing prototypes were built before production of the 57S began in earnest, but even throughout its three year run a mere 17 Atalantes were constructed.

What makes this car rarer still is that a fifth of all the Type 57 cars are in the Musee Nationale de L'Automobile in Mulhouse, France including a quarter of all Atalantes built.

A Bonhams auction company official said, "I have known of this Bugatti for a number of years and, like a select group of others, hadn't dared divulge its whereabouts to anyone. It is absolutely one of the last great barn discoveries, and we at Bonhams are honored to have been selected to handle its sale."

Well, la de da. I, of course, think that's complete balderdash. If you know a valuable car is just sitting there and the family doesn't care about it and hasn't cared about it for decades, you line up your approach, you take a bead on the target, and you give them both barrels, so to speak. Maybe some collectors' excuse might be that "they didn't want to disturb the Doctor," but, if the Doctor cared at all about keeping the reputation of Bugatti alive, there's a good chance he would have enjoyed seeing it out and about, storming around at the Goodwood Revival and such.

I'LL CARRY THE FLAG

My tried-and-true approach, used with success more than once in my barn-finding days, is to say to the car owner, "Hey, tell you what, you sell it to me, I'll fix it up, and I'll come around and give you a ride when it's done." I bought more than one car using that line. Mind you, I didn't always do it because the car was sold before I'd finished restoring it, but when I did go back and visit the former owners of newly spiffed-up cars, the gesture was always very much appreciated—because they secretly knew that, on their own, they would never have gotten around to restoring it.

Another approach might have be to roll up with a brand new car, in this case, say a Bentley, with the title and keys on the seat and say "let's trade." The temptation of having something brand new, still with the "new car smell" can be overwhelming when balanced against a rust ridden hulk buried for 50 years.

So the lessons to be learned here are: 1. Don't be shy, approach that owner. 2. Figure out what the owner wants–maybe it's not just money, but to see someone else carry on the mission, restoring the car the way they would have if they'd had the money and/or energy.

Who knows what it would have taken to get Dr. Carr to part with his 57S? But one thing's sure, in 50 years, nobody tried quite hard enough.

And, by the way, Bonhams sold it for $4.4 million dollars.

Chapter 11
When Potentates Go Topless
(1970 Mercedes-Benz 600 LWB Landaulet)
*Great for showing off if you're a celeb, it's a
body style worth celebrating…*

Question: What do Idi Amin, Nicolae Ceausescu, Kim
Young Dam, Mobutu, Tito, the Sultan of Brunei, the Pope,
and Queen Elizabeth all have in common?

Answer: They all, at one time or another, toodled about in a
Mercedes 600.

This slab-sided monolith was Mercedes' ultimate luxury car
of the Sixties. But from this point on, I speak not of the all-too-
common 600, or even it's "Pullman" version (nicknamed after
the Pullman railroad car), but the 600 landaulet (sometimes
spelled "landaulette"), where the forward section (which I refer
to as the "chauffeur's area") is steel roofed and the rear seat has
its own convertible top.

That car came about after Mercedes failed to unseat Rolls
Royce and Bentley in the luxury car field with its 300 in the

early '50s. When it designed a new generation car for the '60s, Mercedes bent all effort toward making the 600 the best luxury car in the world. If you look at the list of royals and VIPs who owned 600s, Mercedes succeeded. Mercedes' chief engineer, Rudolph Uhlenhaut, would take visitors up on the test track to the banked part of the racetrack called "the wall of death" and do four wheel drifts. Try that in your Rolls PV!

Part of what made it possible was the engine, the V-8 that made the smaller 300SEL the world's fastest production sedan.

That engine was the heart of the 600.

The V-8 boasted mechanical fuel injection, with large, dual air-intake tubes, and a cam atop each cylinder bank. This post-war car was the equivalent of the 770 Grosser flagships of the 1930s. Mercedes built the cars in small quantities each year at Sindelfingen. It was not your everyday car, but a special order car, and was in production a long time, all the way from 1963 to 1981.

The 600 limo started out as a 7/8 passenger 600 sedan first shown at the 1963 Frankfurt Auto Show. The 600 sedan with an overall length of 218.1 inches would eventually become known as the SWB (short wheelbase), while the larger "Pullman" versions had a total length of 245.67 inches.

They were heavy, at 5,300 lbs. but a 600 SWB sedan was capable of cruising in the 125 to 130 mph range. Again, try that in your Rolls Phantom V or VI.

The 0 to 60 mph time was 10 seconds. Alas, fuel consumption was only 9 to 12 mpg, but let's just say that the people who owned 600s weren't the type who need worry about fuel costs.

The four-wheel disc brakes consisted of dual calipers at the front with regular disc brakes at the rear that were power-boosted via the air from the fully independent, self-leveling air suspension. Along with a swing rear axle, and driver-adjustable (via a three-position lever on the steering column) shock absorbers, the 600 used large, for the time, 235/70R15 tires mounted on painted silver steel wheels.

The ground clearance height could be raised automatically

through hydraulics. Five V-belts drove two alternators, the AC, a hydraulic pump, cooling fan, and the air compressor.

These were cars ordered for kings of countries and kings of industries, and custom touches were part of almost every 600 ordered. In addition to your choice of velour or leather interior, sunroof, glass divider between driver and rear seat passengers, refrigerated bars, and other such sundries, flag mounts were available for the front fenders so you could announce to the peasantry who was coming. There were over 50 pieces of real wood trim, a full array of blackout curtains for privacy, and courtesy lights aplenty inside a standard 600.

Power-operated equipment, via hydraulics with pressures up to 300 psi, included all the windows and the interior privacy glass, front and rear seats (the first Mercedes-Benz to get these), sunroof, cowl vent, fuel-filler door, rear trunk lid, and doors in the early models. Interior temperatures were operated through separate warm/cool controls to make it a pleasant ride for both front and rear seat passengers. The stereo controls were duplicated in the rear seat area. There was also an intercom system so you could talk to the driver if you had the divider window up.

For all practical purposes, the 600 was custom built. Oh, it had a three-pointed star, and an engine made at Mercedes, but it was more than a mass-production car.

RARE

A total of 2,667 Mercedes-Benz 600 models were built in its 18 years of production. Of those, 2,190 were short wheelbase (SWB) cars, while another 428 were the stretched (27.6 in. longer) wheelbase versions. Some Pullman models had six doors, but the four-door model was more common.

THE NE PLUS ULTRA: THE LANDAULETTE

In its successful attempt to unseat the Rolls Royce Phantom as the favorite limo of world leaders, Mercedes looked to their museum for inspiration and revived a prewar design—the landaulette (aka landaulet)—that was once common on luxury cars in both England and America before the war. Then, after WWII, it disappeared. Perhaps, in the more Egalitarian spirit that pervaded the U.S. and Europe, this particular design element was thought a bit too pretentious. Imagine, a car where the chauffeur had to drive under a steel roof while his wealthy employers basked in the sun!

The landaulette virtually disappeared from America. But in England, in Rolls Royce Phantom V and even Phantom VI models, there were still landaulettes on the order books, even if they were only ordered by kings, queens, and other dictators of one stripe or another.

So, when Mercedes designers went for a long-wheelbase, stretch-limo version of the 600, they thought, What the hell, Rolls is trying to abandon this market (Rolls was trying to phase out the Phantom VI but, annoyingly, kept getting orders...), let's make a car to fill the void.

Most of these half-open 600 limos were ordered by folk whose wont was to stand up in the rear of the car and wave to the unwashed masses during parades. This was, mind you, before more troubled times led to fear of the well-aimed hand grenade and open parade cars became scarce again. Today, at this writing, only Queen Elizabeth and the ruler of North Korea regularly use their 600 landaulettes.

A mere 59 were made. Naturally, they weighed even more than the steel-roofed —Pullmans: almost 6,000 pounds.

The rear "quarter roof" was hydraulically operated. Some have more open area than others. The ones with the longer soft top, where two thirds of the car's interior can be exposed to the sun, were called "Presidential" models; of which 11 were constructed.

WORLDWIDE HUNTS

The internet has been a great boon to car collectors. It allows the free flow of information, making it possible for fans of a particular car to congregate and hunt together for the object of their affection. I am in debt to the M100 Message Board (found at http://www.m-100.cc/forum/default.aspM100), on which, almost daily, new reports are posted by club members about their progress in the worldwide search for Mercedes 600 cars. As is the case with most forums, there are subgroups. The one after my own heart is the "landaulet" thread, where forum members are treading down some particularly dark alleys on the trail of fallen kings, fled dictators, and other celebrities who have cast aside their golden chariots—the fabled 600 laundaulette.

Perusing page after page of their discoveries, I was drawn to the story of the landaulette of Romanian President Nicolae Ceausescu. Chassis no. 10001512001217, the second of two he owned. It had the added status of being a Presidential model, with the longer convertible top, and of having six doors. Eventually, it came to auction in America.

Flag mounts on the front fenders weren't the only clue this car was a state car and not one built for some anonymous Wall Street tycoon.

No, this car came with an established history as the car of a head of state, though Romanian President Nicolae Ceausescu was hardly someone warmly remembered. From 1967 to 1989, he and his wife spent money like water, at one point building a 1,100-room palace that is bigger than the Pentagon. He treated the revenue of products produced in his country like it was all his to spend, and his family lived like royalty. He even had a royal scepter made. Meanwhile, his secret police were among the most brutal in history. His whole regime was a witch's brew of personality cult, nationalism, nepotism, and poisoned foreign relations. Finally, when he ordered security forces in Timisoara to fire on protesters on December 17, 1989, Romanians could take no more. As the revolt began, Ceaușescu and his wife tried to flee the capital in a helicopter, but were captured by armed rebels. On Christmas day, the couple were tried by a special military tribunal on charges of genocide and sabotage of the Romanian economy. The trial took but two hours. They were then summarily shot.

The auction house charged with finding an owner for Ceausescu's landaulette didn't tell the political story behind the car in their catalog description. While some cars are hyped as having belonged to famous personalities (Elvis, The Queen, etc.), when the personality involved happens to be one of history's bad men, their bios are shortened considerably.

Another deposed dictator whose cars are being followed by members of the M100 Message Board is Mobuto, an African leader who was overthrown in the First Congo War by a man supported by the governments of Rwanda, Burundi, and Uganda.

In 1997, following failed peace talks, Mobutu fled to Togo, but lived mostly in Morocco. He died in September, 1997, in Rabat, Morocco, from prostate cancer. His cars featured on the M100 website, look decidedly worse for wear, more like typical old, used cars than one-time conveyances of heads of state. The M100 site says serial numbers of his landaulettes were 001861 and 001129.

In my humble opinion, the 600 landaulet is one of the hottest Holy Grails on the barn find trail. And, if you read that website, you'll find the hunt is far from over. There are many accounted for, but not all. Dictators are falling everywhere. Keep your powder dry, and your cash ready, and you, too, could be on the first wave in to buy a ruler's toys after he's been deposed.

But a cautionary note is in order. While it is a romantic notion that you can go to some country where a dictator has just been overthrown and buy his most treasured car, I would say it's a fool's errand without local contacts on the winning side. There could be many a slip between the cup and the lip, first in buying the car legally and second in getting it out of the country.

Next problem? Can you bring it into the U.S. if it was not made as a U.S.-certified model? The answer is yes if the car is over 25 years old.

Nevertheless, tracking down a 600 landaulette is, to my mind, one of The Last Great Adventures still awaiting an enthusiast. Bringing one home would be one of the greatest coups you could perform in the collector car world. One of less than 100 made? The ultimate Mercedes of its time? It is to die for

(and, fair warning, you could die trying to get one, in some dark corner of the world...)

It takes a lot of chutzpah to own a car like a 600 landaulette. For one thing, it's too damn big for you to drive yourself. (And do you really want to be mistaken for a chauffeur?). So you will have to have a bloke properly liveried up to take the wheel (and where do you buy a chauffeur's uniform these days?) But it is guaranteed you will have every eye upon you when you pull up to an event. Arriving in a 600 landaulette for your red carpet appearance, you would only have to worry about being upstaged by, say, a Rolls Royce Phantom V landaulette bodied by James Young, maybe one encrusted with crystals (no, no, just kidding—Liberace's P5 landaulette is in storage now that his museum is closed and the man in charge said it's not for sale).

And of course once you have landed it on your own country's turf, you would have to decide which flags to fly on your flag mounts. I think, given my druthers, I'd design my own flag. Make up a country (though I think my family on my father's side has a coat of arms, someplace, in Switzerland).

As an auctioneer once said when they rolled an ex-president's car across the stage: "Stretched limousines have become almost common in most American cities today, but the dignified presence of the 600 will always be noticed, especially one as grand as the ultra-rare 600 Landaulet."

Chapter 12
A Purebred Ferrari Goes Custom in Kiwiland (1955 Ferrari Dino F1)

You see Ugly, ask what's underneath…in this case it was a Ferrari Grand Prix car.

What if you were invited to look at a Ferrari racing coupe and you were absolutely horrified at how grotesque the bodywork was? What do you say if you can't believe anyone would think that the misbegotten contraption in front of you could ever be mistaken for a Ferrari GT car made in Maranello, Italy?

Okay, different scenario: What if you stumble across it in the hinterlands and realize that, although the body was borne of someone's misguided wet dream of a Grand Touring Ferrari, underneath lies a real Ferrari race car, one that, properly re-bodied, would be worth a million bucks?

IT HAPPENED.

In 1960, New Zealand businessman and enthusiast racing driver Pat Hoare made a trip to Italy to purchase a V-12 engine for his Ferrari 625 single-seater (ex-de Portago, Mike Hawthorn, and Frolian Gonzales) to replace its problematic inline-four. Hoare was a personal friend of Enzo Ferrari and, using his clout, had created the so-called "Tasman Special" 625–it had a larger 2,996cc engine–in 1957.

Sometimes you get more than you bargained for. In this case, when Hoare triumphantly returned from Italy, he came back with not just a new V-12 engine, but with a complete Dino 256–Chassis No. 0007, the same car that America's racing hero and Ferrari works driver Phil Hill had piloted to victory at that year's Monza GP. Though it's front-engine design was technically obsolete, that obsolescence turned out to be in the car's favor, appreciation-wise. Ferrari was begrudgingly switching to mid-engine F1 cars at the time, and No. 0007 ended up being the last front-engine car to win a Formula 1 Grand Prix.

Ferrari gamely tried to forestall going mid-engine. Knowing front-engine configurations were obsolete, it nevertheless tried to make up for the car's handling weaknesses by increasing the size of the engine. In 1959, Ferrari enlarged its engine to the 2.5-liter maximum allowed. In addition, this car was updated it with disc brakes, something else Enzo Ferrari had resisted before but finally began experimenting with in 1958.

It was competitive, but just barely. Ferrari drivers had a habit of driving beyond their abilities to please the old man, and he had already lost a lot of his front-line drivers by the time he retained Tony Brooks. Brooks drove the car to second place in the final rankings, behind Australian Jack Brabham in the Cooper-Climax.

But even the best driver couldn't keep the front-engine Dino in front of the British onslaught of mid-engine cars. Brooks carved out a victory for Ferrari in France and Germany, but couldn't match that in the other races. Labor troubles on the home front caused Ferrari to cancel their entry in the British Grand Prix, which they probably could have won, considering Ferraris had taken the first two places only weeks before at the Aintree 200.

TASMAN RULES

Back in New Zealand, the car was more competitive, and Hoare was able to run according to "Tasman" rules, which allowed an engine size up to three liters, so he ran the Dino 246 not with the 2,414cc V6 but with a 2,953cc 60-degree V-12 Testa Rossa motor, one of the engines run by the works 250TR two-seaters. Producing over 330 hp, the V-12 boasted at least 50 hp more than that of the previously employed Dino V-6.

With the new engine, the car had cajones. He qualified the car 14th for the New Zealand GP at Ardmore in January, 1961, and managed to finish 7th behind all the luminaries in GP at the time, including the race winner Jack Brabham, Bruce McLaren, Graham Hill, Ron Flockhart, Denny Hulme, and Jim Clark. Though beat by a mid-engine car, Hoare's Ferrari was the first front-engine car home.

At the next race, Hoare finished 2nd to Hulme at Dunedin, but at that event there were few big name drivers in attendance. At the Teretonga International, he finished fourth behind Jo Bonnier, Roy Salvadori, and Hulme. But at least he finished first overall in the Waimate 50 road race, against all Kiwi drivers.

TRANSFORMATIVE

The car had done well, but was becoming more uncompetitive race by race as mid-engine cars began to fill the grid. It came to the point where, as fisherman say, it was time to fish or cut bait. Hoare decided to cut bait, making the single seater into a robust road car. What was obsolete on the track might be a real kick to drive on the road. What appealed to him stylistically was the 250GTO—not the first incarnation with the fastback, but the second generation Series II Hatchback models with what some refer to as a "sugar scoop" roof (like a 250LM).

The story goes that Ferrari supplied him with blueprints of the '64 GTO, along with the all-important large wrap-around windscreen. But, though there might have been chassis drawings, I don't think those bodies had blueprints—I think Ferrari's metal-benders just hammered out sections for the body, loosely following the shape of a wooden former. Unless Scaglietti sent him the wooden formers, I doubt if Hoare's NZ metal-bender had much of a guide beyond photographs of a 250GTO Series

II. Anybody looking at the measurements of the two cars could have predicted the result would be a misshapen beast, because the 256 had a wheelbase 6 inches shorter than the GTO. Plus Hoare was over 6 feet tall, so he needed to alter the seating position anyway.

After the single-seater bodywork was lifted off and stored, the newly fabricated two-seater body was placed on the chassis, which itself had been changed from center steering to right-hand drive (leaving the gauges on the opposite side of the dash—go figure!).

Hec Green, a New Zealand race car designer and fabricator, is said to be the fabricator of the tube frame that held the body. Local panel beater Reg Hodder, of G. B. McWhinnie and Co., took nine weeks to bend the 16-gauge aluminum over that tubular network. The interior was done by a lad only 18 years old, George Lee.

All the 256 running gear was retained, as were the wheels, brakes, suspension, steering wheel, and even the clear "bubble" on the bonnet that gave bystanders a look at the intimidating row of trumpets topping the six Weber carbs. Those were never on the real GTO's, but that was just one clue this car was a wanna-be GTO.

The car tripped the scales at around 700 kg, which was 200 kg lighter than a genuine GTO, and boasted 30 hp more, thus leading a reporter from one of the British magazines to claim that even Ferrari would consider "this homebuilt [car] to be one of the fastest Ferraris on earth." Ferrari probably didn't take the car seriously, and laughed all the way to the bank. The things those crazy Kiwis do!

Hoare owned it to the time of his death, when it was purchased by Logan Fow, who took part in a number of club racing events and standing sprints, recording a best of 13.9 seconds for the quarter mile. Next it was owned by Donald McDonald, who attempted to break the 3.0-liter New Zealand land speed record in 1969 but came up a smidgen short, with a best top end speed of 155mph (249.6khp). Hardly in a genuine 250GTO's ballpark. They can do about 170mph.

The Ferrari was eventually purchased by Neil Corner, along with all the original 256 bodywork. Corner put the car back into its original single-seater form, the way it was when it arrived in New Zealand. The craftsmen in charge of doing this were Crosthwaite and Gardiner. The only original item that couldn't be used in the restoration was the perspex carburetor cover, which had turned yellow with exposure to sunlight and heat.

After it was restored, it went to the Ferrari Club Italia meet at Imola in '87. Then it went to the Essen Motor Show in '89, and several vintage races at Silverstone. By 2003, it was owned and raced by Tony Smith, who competed in Spa Ferrari Days that year, finishing fifth overall.

I've lost track of where it's been since, but the lesson to be learned here is that, no matter how ugly that makeshift GTO body was, anyone interested in appreciation potential would have been a fool to walk away from it at any reasonable price, for there was a great treasure underneath. And not only that, the original GP body had been saved, so it was not as difficult a transformation back to original as it would've been if the original fuselage style body had been lost. In collector circles today, having the original metal is considered bringing it much more back to original, rather than having a new body fabricated.

So lesson learned? Drag yourself across that racetrack and take a look at those oddball cars, the hodge-podge-looking homebuilts. There could be a world-class car underneath...like there was with this one.

Chapter 13
The Italian Jag
(1967 Jaguar 2+2 Pirana)

Created for a newspaper promotion, the once ugly duckling became a swan...

New car designs come about in strange and mysterious ways. Most often, automakers originate them with their own designers and engineers. But sometimes they come from independent coachbuilders and design firms, who make concepts to display at auto shows, hoping public demand will tip the automaker into coming to them for production versions.

Another way is when somebody outside the auto industry wants something built as a promotional gimmick.

That's how this Italian-bodied Jaguar E-type came about almost five decades ago, when an executive at *The Daily Telegraph* in London thought it would be good promotion for his newspaper if he bankrolled the design of an all-new car. Of course, it would have to be a British chassis. So he got some automotive reporters together and they went over what Ferrari, Lambo-

rghini, and the others were doing, and concluded they needed a rakish sports car.

The budget was something like a third of a million pounds, an unheard of amount for a newspaper promotional gimmick, but, hey, they were creating art!

The reporters eventually decided the Jaguar E-type chassis would be the best one to build on, and, after talking to coachbuilders, chose Bertone Carrozzeria in Bertone to clothe it in a sporty design, giving only the vaguest outline of what they wanted. Starting with a new 4.2-litre 2+2 from Jaguar, Marcello Gandini, the chief designer at Bertone, redesigned it into what the reporters had envisioned as the "ideal car."

By the way, the car was supposed to be called "Piranha," after the very nasty, flesh-eating fish found in South America, but when Bertone found out that name was taken, they shortened it to Pirana. It made its debut at the 1967 London Motor Show at Earl's Court on the stand of Carrozzeria Bertone S.A.S. If anyone hoped that this would be the design Jaguar would choose when doing another generation of E-type, they hoped in vain. Still, despite nobody waving their checkbook, Bertone schlepped it over to the Turin and New York motor shows and the British Motor Show in Montreal.

Stylistically, you could say the design borrows a lot from Bertone's Alfa Romeo prototype for the Montreal. Also, it paved the way for the styling of the Lamborghini Espada, also a front-engine car. Ironically, one of the most outstanding features of the car is wheels from an earlier Jaguar D-type race car, which give it a macho look if you recognize them.

Inside, the car boasted a new interior with a more integrated center console, redesigned seats and new door panels. They also fitted power windows and a powered antenna. Smiths Industries assisted with much of the interior, including a prototype climate control system that fed cool air to the roof and warm air through the floor. Phillips installed an experimental tape player, a forerunner to the cassette tape.

After the hubbub of being a show car died down, the car was

sold by the *Telegraph* for a reported $30,000, a fraction of its development cost. But by then the newspaper was off promoting something else, and the car was just an old car gathering dust down in their car park. Exactly how it got to America is unknown, but, interestingly, your author was going by a used-car lot in Palm Springs several decades later and spotted it. I pulled over and was told it would be around $75,000.

I thought it a bargain for a hand-built prototype, but it would have been a bit of a stretch for me at the time. A few years later, I read that it had been bought by Ed Superfon, the onetime owner of the VIP Car Store, an exotic car lot in Santa Monica that I used to visit frequently in the '70s, only he says he paid several times that. Perhaps it had an intermediate owner or two. At any rate, Mr. Superfon restored it and has shown it at many events, including Concorso Italiano.

There's a couple lessons to be learned here. One is that, once the limelight was off the car, you could have guessed the newspaper was open to offers on last year's promotional gimmick—and they got one. My excuse was I wasn't hunting for the car. Now on that second buying opportunity in Palm Springs, I could have bargained with the dealer, maybe got a payment plan going, but I wasn't sure if it was a prototype generated from within the coachbuilder or some outside proposal that was built to a design that came from outside.

Now I have to say it's an outside proposal, because the newspaper funded it and thought it up, but without seeing evidence of drawings sent over from the newspaper, I don't know how much freedom Gandini had in designing the shape. I, myself, prefer a prototype conceived of and built right at the carrozzeria with no outside influences, like the Bertone Rondine, built on a '63 Corvette chassis. Even if GM gave them the Corvette chassis, GM had no input in the design.

Still, when Jaguars are displayed at concours d'elegance in the future, the Pirana will be a most welcome car. So the main lesson to be learned is that, yes, you can buy prototypes. This one is not my cuppa tea, but it's still a significant car...

Chapter 14
Don't Cry for Me, Argentina, Disappearing Alfa
(1953 Alfa Romeo 3000CM)
Some people think that the split-window Corvette design originated on the '63 Stingray...

Not so. It was on an Alfa way back in 1955, some eight years before the "Aerovette" (as Bill Mitchell, GM's Styling VP, called it) made its debut as a 1963 Corvette.

And here's the kicker: the car design was commissioned by the husband of the most famous woman ever to come from Argentina—Eva Peron.

Yes, the svelte, blonde wife of the dictator, the same one that, decades later, inspired the Broadway musical "*Evita.*"

And here's how it happened.

FROM LE MANS TO ARGENTINA

Juan Peron was an aficionado of the first order. He reportedly gave Boano, the coachbuilder, a commission to do an Alfa for him on a 6C 3000 CM (*Competizione Maggiorata*) race-car chassis.

First a little bit of background on the 3000 CM. They were

built as works cars for the factory to contest Europe's biggest events, like the Mille Miglia and Le Mans, and most experts agree that 3000 CMs were the ultimate version of the 6C race cars. Although they used a 3.5-liter engine, they actually had a lineage that goes back to the pre-war 6C 1750 and the later 6C 2500 SS race cars.

The 3000 CM immediately trailed the 6C 2500 *Competizione,* but produced nearly double the horsepower with its much larger engine. Both used the 6C's independent suspension, but had a shorter wheelbase than the production cars.

Three or four coupes were bodied by Colli for the 1953 Mille Miglia. Despite competition from Lancia and Ferrari, one of the coupes finished second overall. Later, the cars were brought to Le Mans, where they recorded the highest top speed of 154 mph down the Mulsanne straight. Unfortunately, all three cars DNFed.

Following Le Mans they were just used race cars. At least three were rebodied.

One got a Zagato Coupe, and that went to Swedish race driver Joakim Bonnier. Another—chassis 1361.00126-1953—was sent to Carrozzeria Boano for a new body and gifted to Argentinian president Juan Peron, who fancied it as a road car. A third went to Carrozzeria Pininfarina where it served as the basis for the Superflow concept car.

Boano's design was pretty slick, including the two-piece rear window, wrapping around to the sides like the 1963 Corvette.

But, by creating it, a little bit of history was lost, because this car had, in fact, participated in the 24 hours of Le Mans in 1953, and the driver there was the most famous driver from Argentina, *mi amigo* Juan Manuel Fangio (our picture together is in the jacket of my book *De Tomaso: The Man and his Machines*). It is rumored that Fangio had pretty much bent the body anyway, so it was removed and the new, more street-like body was laid on.

The new design borrowed a lot from the Disco Volante (flying saucer) show cars designed by Touring.

THE GEARHEAD DICTATOR

The car was reported as a gift to Peron from the Argentina General Labor Confederation (CGT); and it is still being argued today who paid for it. You like to think Peron had labor on his side, if they were so generous with presents. But, the fact is, Peron's wretched excesses rankled the working class and led to his later overthrow.

Perón sported the car about in public, most notably at the Autodromo de Buenos Aires, where Perón drove three laps before a race. But then he or some driver who worked for him had a little run-in with a bus and the Alfa lost. So an Italian craftsman, Alberto Borghi, was retained to straighten out the car.

But the political situation was getting dicey. On September 16, 1955, Perón was forced to flee to nearby Paraguay and all his property was confiscated and auctioned off to the highest bidder. Among his four-wheel treasures were a Ferrari 212 Inter with coachwork by Ghia, an Alfa Romeo 1900 CSS with coachwork by Touring, and a Giulietta Sprint.

An American who must have been tuned in to Peron's cars, a man named William Decker, bought the 6C at the auction and then sold it to a local Argentinian, Carlos Lostaló, a Maserati race-car driver. Then that driver sold it to another Maserati man, Roberto Mieres.

In 1967, Argentine J.M. Ahumada (said to be a mere go-between) sold the car for $10,500 through the Vintage Car Store in Nyack, New York.

It left Argentina in 1968, and the next known owner was Mr. Ed Bond of Connecticut. Bond kept the car for a few years, but eventually sold it in 1970 to Henry W. Wessells, III.

Hank was a collector of the first order. He worked for the Budd Company in Detroit, a major supplier to the auto industry (for instance, they built the bodywork for the two-seat Thunderbirds) and from 1974 to 1977 Hank was the Budd Company's technical representative in Europe, a post that allowed him to live with his family outside of Paris. When he came back, he was posted to Detroit (which, even as a native Detroiter, I hafta say is like being posted to Outer Siberia compared to Paris!) and then worked for three more years to retire early so he could focus on what he really wanted to do: vintage racing.

From 1953 through 2003, Henry was founder and recording secretary of a Philadelphia area club, The Clots, that was dedicated to the enjoyment of vintage motoring. He raced in North America, England, and continental Europe. Alfa Romeo's own historians regularly consulted with him on design, technical, and aesthetic matters, and Alfa collectors the world over relied upon him to evaluate the authenticity of their cars regarding the accuracy of their restoration.

THE CAR MEETS A TREE

With the car in its Boano body—painted black—Wessells raced it at various events for a decade and a half until 1984, when he hit a tree at the Pittsburgh Vintage Grand Prix. I could ask what trees were doing on a racetrack, but, suffice to say, the body was wrecked beyond repair. Wessells had it restored in England, then went on to race at events like the LeMans Classic.

The car was eventually owned by Larry Auriana.

So, now we come back to the Eternal Question: in which class should concours judges evaluate this car? Should we strict constructionists insist it have a coupe body like the one in which it was "born" within '53? Or should it have the rarer and more beautiful one-off Boano-style body it had when it was a road car? Or is it correct for a race car to have different bodies at different times, just as the livery changes as the car moves from team to team? I say the latter interpretation is the most liberal, allowing a chassis to sport bodies it has worn on different occasions for different purposes, so long as its current looks can be documented to be a body style it wore "in period," documentation which this car has.

Lesson to be learned here? The absolute best time to buy this car was when it was in Argentina, after it crashed. There were no craftsmen in Argentina who could repair it, and it was already an obsolete car as far as racing. But even when Hank Wessells crashed it a second time, it would have been a bargain. Owners of crashed cars (if they survive) often just want to get the car out of their lives. So it's your duty as a barn finder to follow vintage racing, get business cards from everyone you meet at every event, and keep an ear to the ground on what's happening with their cars.

I remember one time I went to a hillclimb in Michigan, oh, about 1965. A D-type Jag hit a tree on its way up the hill and the event was cancelled. The thought didn't even occur to me: where did the wreck go? I should have followed the tow truck, after first stopping to get my checkbook. By the way, last time I looked, D-types were over a million dollars...

Chapter 15
The (First) Elvis 507
(1957 BMW 507)

He threw Mercedes for a loop when "The King" (of rock 'n roll) bought a BMW while stationed in Germany

Now here is a story that attempts to separate fact from fiction. Elvis Presley bought a BMW 507. True. His co-star on a film, Swiss star Ursula Andress, was given a BMW 507 by Elvis. Also true.

But the source of endless confusion is that these were two different cars. The one Elvis owned was a former race car driven by German racing legend Hans Stuck. The one he gave Ursula was *another* 507 he gifted her with after she turned down a Cadillac, saying a Cad "wouldn't fit her life style" (if, indeed, people said that back in 1963...)

The film they worked on together was the1963 classic *Fun in Acalpulco*. They frolicked on the beach in the film, but we don't know if the frolicking continued offstage. After all, each of them was at the time already married to someone else! After the film, he wanted to give her a memento, and that was BMW 507 No. 70192.

One intrepid reporter following this story earlier had heard Andress's husband, John Derek, had given her the car, not Elvis. We have to congratulate the reporter for actually calling her up in Rome and finding out that the car had, indeed, come from Elvis. Decades later, it was one of the featured cars at a 2011 RM auction.

The catalog mentioned a few mods done by none other than North Hollywood's greatest customizer, George Barris, who had put on different bumpers (what you might call hot-rod-style "nerf bars" out on the Coast) and, horrors, Barris plastered her picture all over the dashboard!

The car went to auction without the nerf bars, but the main crime against it—having the 507 engine yanked out and a Ford 289 V-8 stuck in—had been corrected years earlier, when an owner put in a 507 engine with a different number than the car had when new. Fortunately, a later owner acquired the original engine and there are plans to put it back in the car.

Why did the movie star sell the car? Well, because that's what movie stars do. They often start out poor, hit it big, buy a lot of stuff, and then the time comes when they get so much stuff they have to put it in storage. Sometimes they sell the stuff cheap rather than pay storage. She was lucky she got full value (at that time) for the car, selling it to George Barris for $10,000.

So if you are an Ursula Andress buff, you are happy with that car. But if you are an Elvis buff, you will have to carry the torch for a car now owned by Jack Castor, who wrote in *Bimmer* magazine #63 that he was the car's owner, and that it had been stored just down the coast from Bimmer HQ for almost 40 years.

In that issue, it is explained that the ex-Hans Stuck ex-Elvis car was, indeed, a former race car. Chassis No. 70079 was completed in Munich on September 13, 1957. It then went on display at the 1957 Frankfurt show. Hans Stuck used it to take automotive writers for hair-raising rides, but the racing was real, too. Stuck won three hillclimbs with it in 1958. It was refurbished at BMW toward the end of that year, and on December 12 it was delivered to Autohaus Wirth in Frankfurt, Germany, where it caught the eye of Elvis Aaron Presley, former Tupelo Mississippi truck driver, and, oh, yes, a crooner riding the tidal wave of rock and roll.

The car came to the U.S. in 1960, coincidentally the same year that Elvis returned to the U.S. after a two-year stint in Germany. But while it was presented in New York as "Elvis's 507," there's no hard evidence that Elvis himself imported it, or that he ever drove a 507 on U.S. soil. So all the publicity pictures of Elvis in the car are for naught apparently, if you wanted to use them to establish US ownership. Those were all taken in Germany, mostly while he was wearing his enlisted man's dress uniform. The car was purchased by radio personality Tommy Charles, who brought it to Alabama and modified it extensively by throwing out the BMW 507 V-8 and stuffing in a Chevy V-8 engine and, oh yes, doing a custom interior.

Not long after, it ended up in the basement of an Atlanta BMW dealership, where a young Air Force pilot named Lloyd Cottle traded a Ferrari GTE and $1,500 for it in 1966. (From our viewpoint 50 years later, this may have been a mistake.) Two years later, Cottle sold it to Jack Castor, its current owner, who drove it for a few years with its Chevy drivetrain. In 1973 Castor took it off the road, hoping to reunite it with a BMW V-8 and the correct transmission.

Elvis 507, Chassis No. 70079, was returned to the Munich plant in July, 2014, following a short stint on display at the BMW Museum. It was scheduled for a two-year restoration on behalf of its American owner and finally shown at Pebble Beach where no doubt some were not aware that it was once property of The King. (They could have at least put a teddy bear on the seat, teddy bears with an Elvis "thing.")

Lesson to be learned? Again, celebrities buy cars. Again, celebrities dump cars. Your job is to be there when they lose interest in them, or when the public has forgotten the celebrity and he or she really needs the money. Even though BMW 507s were not exactly sought after compared to their competition at the time, the Mercedes 300SL roadster, the name "Elvis" being tied to this car no doubt helped it avoid the crusher.

Love me tender, El...

Chapter 16
The Swap Meet Porsche
(1964 Porsche 901)
Hey, you go with knowledge, you find treasure....

The Pomona Swap meet, which occurs several times a year, is a famous meet. First of all, it's about 40 miles East of Los Angeles, held on a vast parking lot and there's every sort of car there from beat-up VW Beetles to Rolls Royces, but mostly there are vendors with parts rusting away in the noonday sun. You wouldn't think that you could find a valuable Porsche there. But I'm here to tell you that you have to be a contrarian. You might not find a Porsche, but if you do, you have to figure that not everybody that goes there is in fact educated in Porsches. Oh they know there's the upside-down bathtub-shaped cars, the 356s, and then there's the wedgier-shaped 911s but that's about it.

So it is in this mindset that I bring you back to that fateful morning in November 1986 when Kurt Schneider and his wife, Lori, were spending the morning at the Pomona Swap Meet when what he called "a life-changing event took place." They found a

1966 Porsche that turned out to be a 1964 Porsche 901 coupe.

Now this is somewhat earthshaking in Porsche terms because most people think the 911 didn't exist until 1965 and most people in the general public had never heard of the *Typ* 901. Now the Schneiders were not uneducated. Kurt wrote in a story on the Beverly Hills Porsche website (where the car's display at the dealer was shown) that he and his wife had joined PCA two years before, after purchasing their first Porsche, and considered themselves to be "active Porschephiles." And they thought of the Pomona Swap Meet as a "happy hunting ground" so much so that they had in advance blocked out all the swap meets to come for the whole year on their calendar. They dutifully read *Panorama* (a Porsche magazine) cover to cover. But the real stroke of luck, and as good an example of any of the truth of the old saw "Luck is what happens when preparation meets opportunity" they had a few weeks prior to the Swap Meet read an article about the oldest known existing 901 in the U.S., at that time being serial number 300032, a car which was actively involved in vintage racing.

Now this couple was what you call "numbers minded" so even though they didn't carry that article with them they had that serial number–300032 — etched on their brains as the earliest 911 found. So it was that, while strolling through the Porsche section of the swap meet, where cars were both on display (you could say it's a "concours for the disadvantaged," there being no judges and no rules…)and for sale, they saw a bright red 911 with a "For Sale" sign. Now the sign read 1966 911S, $4600."

A SELLER THAT KNOWS FROM NUTHIN'

After making a cursory examination of the car they silently noted several things that were pre-dating any 911 they had even seen. That was their first clue that this was a barn finder's dream because you want a seller who knows from nuthin'. If he starts quoting you factory serial numbers chapter and verse, he knows too much for you to ever get a good deal. But this guy didn't even know what year his car was. They could hear the angels singing…

Now it turns out there's a perfectly good reason why this car was mis-labeled a 911. At that point in time when they started production, in 1964, Porsche didn't have its act together on getting cars over to the U.S. They might have labeled it a 1966 Porsche by the time it was sold at the dealer's. Also it might have been self imported (that was before the emissions and DOT and NHTSA regulations kicked in) and the model year changed then. Plus there is the problem of the 901 number, when Porsche updated it to a 911 number they might have at that time affixed the 1966 date. *Wikipedia* says the 901 was presented at the *Internationale Automobil*-Ausstellung (Frankfurt Motor Show) in Frankfurt in September 1963, ... They say: "It took several more months until the cars were manufactured for sale to customers. Between 14 September and 16 November 1964, 82 cars were built and the 901 was presented in October at the 1964 Paris Auto Salon." Wikipedia further says: "Officially the 901s already constructed were used for testing and for exhibitions, and Porsche sold none to private customers. Nevertheless, several of the cars retained by Porsche at that time appear to have made it to private ownership subsequently: in 2010 it was reported that car number 37 was owned by a Porsche specialist named Alois Ruf."

The Schneiders noticed it was an early car, and didn't have, for example, any indentations for decals in the engine compartment –something they had seen on all the other early 911 cars they had seen. Then Kurt noticed the lack of rocker panel trim, the four screw horn grilles (at least on one side), and the "different looking" wood trim across the dash. Playing Sherlock Holmes, he asked to see the front compartment to check for rust, but admitted in an article on the Porsche dealer's website that the request was a bit of subterfuge, because he was in fact "really in search of the Porsche's serial number." He knew from the article on the other early 901 that "while VIN number plates are riveted to the early cars in three places, the serial number is also stamped in the vehicle in the front compartment, pretty close to the heater compartment door." The seller shrugged and said "Take a look" and Kurt Schneider did. He opened the front lid and saw stamped there the number 300020 which was 12 numbers before the car he and his wife had read about as the "oldest existing 911."

ABOUT THE NUMBERS

I asked the eagle-eyed readers on *Pelican Porsche 911 Technical Forum* about the numbers and one, Bob Fleming responded Sept. 21, 2016 with these cogent comments:

"The 901 model number was in use until the end of Thursday Nov 5, it totals 82 cars having the 901 Model name, no cars were finished on Friday or Monday. The following Tuesday Nov. 10, is the first entry for a model 911, that car was a special black metallic (with a gold flake) built for Ferry Porsche. That first 911 is car 300 049. It was the single car completed that day. Remember the cars are not finished in order and a car requiring special attention would have been put to the side for needed attention or parts. Notice the 83rd car completed was serial number 049. Thru the end of the year there were 232 cars completed. That is why a special Registry for these cars - "Early 911 Porsche 232 Registry" has existed since 1985. There are about 75 cars still remaining in the World, plus 30 remaining engines and 5 transmissions (sans bodies). The Kurt and Lori Schneider car 300 020 was given a 1968 year of registration because it's engine, when first registered in California, was a 1968 engine (not the year they bought the car). The car was brought to the US as a used car. They found the car in the 1980's. There is a document (sent) from Porsche to all it's US dealers that the registration of all cars from 300 001 would be registered in the USA as a model year 1966, the first official year the cars were "officially" imported into the country. Remember the 356 was the car that was made beyond 1965 to fill all the orders that were in line, making 1965 the largest sales year of it's 17-year history. By the way many books give the quantity (for) 1964 as 235 cars - that is in error. Car 300 235 was the serial number of the first car off the line in 1965. The quantity of cars completed in 1964 was 232."

NOTE ON BARGAINING

It behooves you at times, when presented the Holy Grail on a red velvet pillow, to restrain yourself from showing any emotion. Look up the phrase "poker faced" and practice in the mirror until you get it down. Schneider was a pro. He pretended he wasn't excited. He said he'd ask his wife. (The seller should have been suspicious right then and there, because what guy's wife is going to know more about cars than the guy?)

Then Schneider threw out a "downer" opinion. You have to be careful in running down a car in hope of getting a lower price–do it wrong and that could kill your chance of making any offer, but it's worth a try at times. He left mumbling about a lot of rust and went to the nearest refreshment stand to get a beer and plan his next move. He had picked the right partner when he married his spouse. She wanted the car as much as him. Now the strategy, as he revealed in his article on the Porsche Beverly Hills website, was to go back, not looking either too anxious or too stupid. They threw an intermediary in there—saying they wanted it but what they would pay depended on what their "mechanic" would say after he checked out the car. Even before the mechanic looked at it they had a "either/or" price range, their starting offer being $4000 with a top tier offer of $4300 tops if the mechanic approved. An appointment was made with the owner at his home a few hours later. Now part of the problem here is, it's Sunday, and if you're doing swap meet buying, can you get your hands on cash on a Sunday (see final chapter for that discussion). They could have said "We're leaving town, we need it now," but that might have tipped off the seller he had a Holy Grail car. So they went home and called up a good friend, identified as Bob Cutshaw, a Porsche expert, owner of a 1965 911 and explained the situation. They told Cutshaw they, in fact, didn't give a damn about the rust or the mechanical condition, they were just intent on correctly identifying the car's age. Everything else, relatively speaking, was unimportant. Cutshaw agreed to check it out if they could drive the 50 miles to his house.

Now to show you this was the good old days, the seller agreed to let them drive the car (sellers; don't do this in modern times!). They drove the car which was very loose, almost dangerously so, and got there under their own steam. Their expert looked over, under, around and through the car and told them it was the real deal. The inspector even made a joke to Schneider that he could simply cut out the number after he bought the car, weld that onto another car and sell that one as No. 20. (Just a joke, purists, don't faint dead away!). They got the car back to the seller with check in hand, got the car, the keys , pink slip (nickname for ownership title in California) and transfer documents and headed home in what they thought at the time was the oldest known 901, maybe even older than anything Porsche had in their museum. One way they were able to get the car restored at a bargain price was to go to a shop they chose, in Reno, where the shop would work at the restoration at a discounted rate given if the car was low priority, as "fill-in" work. And they saved more money by doing the disassembly themselves. They also took pictures as it was dis-assembled as a guide to what goes where in the re-assembly.

The car was rusty. Make no mistake about that. Once the floor pan was removed it was found to be pop riveted sheet metal with resin floated over it. One of the door panels had been repaired with a flattened Coors beer can after some other misadventure. They figured the poor car had been parked on an ice bed in winter, and the rocker panels were full of silt. No less than everything below about 6 inches up the side of the body needed to be refabricated (no panels were available, so refabrication was necessary).

One goof was when the shop tried to repair a dent in the gas tank and ended up "exploding" it – a $2000 goof up which they absorbed), I can't give you a total price on the resto but they overshot the estimate by $6000. Schneider was still happy with the result and it helped that, during the restoration, word was spread that an old, old 901 was found and the car's potential value was mushrooming.

The car was restored and eventually sold. It is now an extremely valuable car for those whose goal to have the earliest 911 possible…but now it exists for all us barn finders as a good object lesson that sometimes people can own something and have absolutely no idea of what they have….

Chapter 17
The Elvis Rolls
(1967 Rolls Royce Phantom V, James Young)
He kept the Mulliner, the chump...

I remember Elvis. Hell, I remember when he was still a Tupelo, Mississippi, truck driver who had recorded a song for his momma on her birthday (*Don't Be Cruel* or maybe *Hound Dog*?). I remember when he was scheduled to be on the *Ed Sullivan Show*, and there was a nationwide debate on whether they should have a long shot showing his pelvis. He was called "Elvis the Pelvis" and could move that thing. They decided to only show him from the waist up.

When he made it big, he had a Rolls Royce Silver Cloud and a Phantom V, one of the big, bloated Mulliner limos. But I didn't know until recently he also had a Phantom by a much better coachbuilder: James Young.

The Phantom V was based on the Silver Cloud II, sharing its newly developed V-8 mated to a four-speed automatic gearbox based on the General Motors Hydramatic design. The chassis followed the general Silver Cloud layout, but had to be lengthened and strengthened because of the increased weight. It was meant to be chauffeur driven.

Only 516 were made, between 1959 and 1968. Park Ward, a one-time independent coachbuilder absorbed by Rolls Royce, made 156. In 1962, H.J. Mulliner and Park Ward were merged by Rolls Royce, forming Mulliner-Park Ward; it accounted for 152 bodies. Prior to the merger, only eight Phantom Vs had been made by H.J. Mulliner.

James Young still stayed independent, long enough to body 195 Rolls Royces, some of these being finished as Sedanca de Villes (with a removable roof over the driver compartment), and they even did one two-door Coupe. Frua in Italy did two, but those are horrendous, and not worth mentioning in polite company.

The Elvis PV, which Bonhams described as the Touring Limousine style (Design PV22) was sold at an auction at the Quail Lodge on August 15, 2014, for a mere $396,000. I was amazed at this, because today they are worth about $450,000 and up in good condition. I'm talking James Young models here, not Mulliner, the much more common PV coachbuilder, and one whose designs I think pale by comparison.

Of course, El's James Young PV wasn't the original color, which might have taken it down a point or two. Legend has it that he was forced to paint it silver so his mother's chickens would stop pecking at it (they thought another chicken was looking at them, so they attacked). The auction company pointed out that he had bought it new, and even showed a bill of sale from Peter Satori, the authorized Rolls dealer in Pasadena.

The car has a few custom touches including a cellular telephone or whatever they called mobile phones in the days of tubes and whatnot. The gray-and-lime cloth upholstery is wretched in color, but probably not as bad as all the pink in his Memphis home.

It didn't go straight from The King to Bonhams. It was first donated to charity on July 4th, 1968, when Elvis gifted it to the SHARE charity, which, at the Santa Monica Civic Auditorium sold it in an auction, raising $35,000. This was after he had owned it for five years.

Elvis was a big-time car fan, owning, at one time or another, a Stutz Blackhawk, several Jaguars, and a BMW507, which he bought while a GI in Germany.

Seeing how Rolls Royce Phantom V limos have climbed in value, this one was a fantastic bargain at $396,000. More so because it was a James Young bodied Phantom V.

I think the next time that same PV James Young limo goes up for auction, they need a life-size statue of the King, and a little of his music playing in the background, maybe *Are You Lonesome Tonight...*

Chapter 18
Requited Love
(1961 Ferrari 250GT California Spyder)

Toly loved his Zagato Ferrari but other collectors loved what was underneath even more…

We hear a lot about unrequited love (see Shakespeare…) but requited love means you loved someone and you got loved back. This is the story of a requited love. Assuming, of course, you can love something mechanical.

Which I say you can, having loved my GTC/4 (see Incredible Barn Finds, Vol. 1). In this case, our story involves an Oklahoma car buff who is more than your average enthusiast. He can recite, for example, from memory, serial numbers of Zagato cars of the'50s and '60s merely by seeing pictures of them. He was an authorized Ferrari dealer at the time. He loves Zagatos from Italy. Which, I should add, is a helluva long way from Oklahoma.

THE CAR UNDERNEATH

We are talking here not just about a Ferrari he coveted, but one clothed by his favorite coachbuilder, Zagato. He first saw this car in 1971 at an Italian auto show. The Oklahoman, Toly Arutunoff, tells the story in his own words (from an e-mail to the author):

I tried to buy it when it was first shown--i was a Ferrari dealer at the time. but i was told 'is not for the sale. it is for the show,' i climbed all over the car; everyone else seemed to be avoiding the Zagato stand. finally the young man in charge gave me a couple of stickers and a lapel badge with that streamline red blue and gold z motif that i haven't seen since. the following year i rushed back to the zagato stand.

Where's the 3z? 'is sold of course,' i was told. Oh, those crazy eighties…

When Arutunoff finally bought this car, he bought it for the shape and was blasé about the fact that under its svelte body was a Ferrari chassis, which had started out life in Maranello as a different model, one that, through the years he owned it, was steadily increasing in value. Actually, not just steadily but by leaps and bounds.

That car was originally a Pininfarina-designed, Scaglietti-built, 250GT Pininfarina Spyder.

In fact, it was the 17th of 56 "short-wheelbase" California Spyders built. It was issued a "Certificato d'Origine," which is sort of its birth certificate, on July 13th, 1961. It had been ordered new by a Sig. Attilio Cupido of Portofino, Italy and was sold to him by the Ferrari Concessionaire, PARAUTO.

As a PF Spyder, it had covered headlights (some Spyders didn't), hotter cams, velocity stacks on the Webers (*Press d'aria*

Trombette, if you want to know the Italian phrase), optional Abarth exhausts, a big 100-liter fuel tank, and metric gauges.

THE CHINETTIS ENTER, STAGE LEFT

Now how did this car go from PF Spyder to Zagato one-off? Well, to learn that story we have to go back in time, to when two figures were still very influential on the Ferrari stage in America: the Chinettis, father and son, both with the first name Luigi. The son thought he was a car designer, and true to this ambition, commissioned several Ferraris to be rebodied. In this case, once the younger Chinetti had approved the design on paper by Zagato, in 1969, the PF Spyder was sold by Cupido to Luigi Chinetti and shipped to Carrozzeria Zagato, in Turin, Italy. The goal was to make the Turin Motor Show in October of 1970 with the all-new design. But, alas, after many a meeting where young Lou Chinetti, Jr., ordered changes to what had already been wrought in metal, the car didn't make it.

Flash forward to October, 1971, and the Turin Motor Show, where it finally graced the stand. The car was given the name "3Z" by Zagato.

Design credit goes to Giuseppe Mittino who, from 1970 on, was Zagato's design director.

The main appeal of the car, compared to the '50s Pininfarina design, was its very geometric shape and hidden headlights. Some say it looks like a sister car to the Alfa Junior Z, the first "wedge" car of many wedges to come.

Ironically, once the car got a new body, the Ferrari scribes, not all of whom could be classified as history professors, began to muck up what chassis it was built on. Some wrong guesses were a "short wheelbase berlinetta," or "short wheelbase competition berlinetta." But, if they had troubled themselves to check the paperwork, they would have said, "no siree, this car was originally a short-wheelbase California Spyder!" Lou Chinetti, Jr., couldn't wait to get the car to the United States. He had a customer just right for it—a local doctor from Long Island, New York. Chinetti was assuming that, once one trend setter had a Zagato Ferrari, other customers would want one, too. And he had several in the works.

Well, we are assuming the doctor liked it. But he was not in love. There's a difference between "like" and "love."

ENTER THE OKLAHOMAN

Let me have Toly himself tell the story, from an e-mail in February 2015:

> *I was sitting at my desk in '79 sorting through my mail, when the Holy Spirit said "You still think about that 3Z. Put an ad in the* New York Times.*" (Yes I'm one of those people). But that meant I'd have to get off my butt and drive about 6 miles (three on expressway) and actually buy a copy of that socialist rag. So I called Stan Nowak. I was surprised when he said he knew where the car was. He said that, as he made some of his income from finding cars, would a 5% finder's fee be acceptable? I agreed--did we need legal documents and such? He said no, he'd trust me for it. I said okay, and he said, "The car's advertised in the* New York Times.*" So not driving 6 miles cost me $2,500.*

The actual ad, run by Concours International Motors of Glen Head, New York, in an April, 1979, edition of the *New York Times*, was headlined "RARE 1966 ZAGATO CONVERT-IBLE All Aluminum-one of a kind." They must have forgotten they had a Ferrari, because the next week they ran a similar ad, only this time identifying it as a Ferrari—but misspelling the name of the coachbuilder: "1966 FERRARI ZUGATO CON-VERTIBLE-1 of kind." In May, 1979, Artunoff flew out to New Yawk City, bought the car for $50,000, and it was love at second sight, the car looking only a tiny bit more worn than it was eight years before.

THE REDISCOVERY

Eight years pass. In 1987, a European automobile historian and author, John de Boer, takes the time to write Ferrari about this car's origin and gets a letter back that identifies the serial number properly:

2491 25SWB Spider Scaglietti "California" 2400mm telio 539, motore Tipo 168 N.2491GT(N. Int.___) cambio 539 N. 539/105, ponte tipo 539.671 N. 358F (8/32) con autobloccante, Borrani 6.00 x 16 13.7.61 Certificato d'Origine Attilio Cupido – GE 1972 transformata in Spider "3Z" dalla Zagato (blu metallizzato) Luigi Chinetti Salone Torino 1971

So de Boer, in 1994, puts that info on page 139 of his Italian Car Registry. He further added the owner's name and the fact it had a personalized OK License plate. "ExSWB3Z"

Suddenly the Ferrari collector world—those beating the bushes for California Spyders, anyway— is brought to attention. The 3Z is now in the limelight. In 1997, Arutunoff was invited to bring the car to the official Ferrari Factory 50th Anniversary celebration. While there, the head of the Ferrari Factory Historic Archive Department, Jean Sage, sees the car and in later correspondence writes this message:

Dear Mr. Arutunoff,
Following my fax dated 22-3-97, I would like to inform you that your car 2491 is not a berlinetta short wheelbase but a spyder California delivered by the GENOA (Italy) dealer to Mr. Attilio CUPIDO of Portofino on July 21, 1961. This information to contradict Mr. H. RABB chassis number list which claims it is was a berlinetta! Best regards, Jean Sage

Sage had to do that clarification because yet another Ferrari documentarian had claimed in a book that it was a coupe when born. Kind of reminds you of those old '50s sword fighting movies where someone was an heir to the royal family, and gets kicked out into the cold and has to not only fight their way back in but prove they are of royal blood (not easy before DNA...)

Arutunoff sold the car to a dealer in northern San Diego for what he says was "many times" what he paid for it. He also had found that Chinetti had originally paid $10,000 for the car and a mere $5,000 to have it bodied by Michelotti. The San Diego dealer, decades later, inspected all the serial numbers, even on steering boxes and other parts, and confirmed it was a short-wheelbase 250GT California Spyder s/n 2491 when built in July, 1961. The car was advertised in 2008 by the dealer for what they claimed was "half the price of other 250GT SWB California Spyders at $3,495,000."

The car was rebodied by a later owner into a California Spyder, not a low-cost task (estimate: $250,000 for bodywork alone—of course, the car later sold for several million).

Lesson to be learned? That sometimes you wonder, when you see a guy fall in love, what in blue blazes he sees in that gal? Well, Toly saw something, and was rewarded for his infatuation. He was rewarded again when others envisioned the car once again in its original body style and paid him handsomely to let it go.

Don't overlook that car with the strange bodywork over in the corner, it could be solid gold underneath. This one sure was...

Chapter 19
Diana Dors and her even more shapely Art Deco Delahaye
(1949 Delahaye 175S)
Never in history have a car and its owner been more ideally matched.

Fact was, we had beautiful blonde actresses before cars got shapely, back in the 1920s. But this is a case where French coachbuilt design reached a nadir of incomparable flamboyance, with some cars built just prior to WWII that were so baroque and "over the top" that, if you saw one go by your table at an outdoor cafe, you almost stood up and cheered.

Actually this Saoutchik-bodied Delahaye, No. 815023, was built after the war, so it was a last attempt to recapture the firm's hold on prewar elegance. Delahaye and Delage were the two French luxury automakers most intertwined with the coachbuilders doing the advanced shapes –rivals Saoutchik and Figoni et Falaschi.

THE STARLET WITH A STAR'S CAR

Now one would have to say that the car was a "star's car" but in 1951, 20-year old Diana Mary Fluck, (known to the world as "Diana Dors") was still more of a starlet hoping to be a star. She was Britain's answer to Marilyn Monroe, but maybe with more curves (36D-24-35 if you hounddogs *must* know)

History credits her third husband, Dennis Hamilton, with

finding this shapely Delahaye in Paris, already painted a fantastic turquoise blue. And the price was £6000 (also reported as Pounds Sterling 5000) –enough to buy a three-bedroom house back in London. But Hamilton knew the car would be ideal photo material as a prop for his zaftig 20-year old wife, so he sprung for it. The press went ga-ga over it as well, exaggerating the car's features—saying it had "gold plated dashboard fittings and a "crystal" steering wheel.

The Type 175 S was one of just 51 built up to 1951, in the firm's waning years before it was taken over by Hotchkiss. The reason it has such a long bonnet is because it was powered by 4456cc straight-six, with a seven-main-bearing crankshaft. Under the hood, the exotica continued with triple Solex carburetors. It was rated at 160 bhp. The chassis had a Dubonnet front suspension with a de Dion tube and parallel semi-elliptic springs at the rear. Brakes were hydraulic with finned alloy drums.

Back in the late pre-war period you first ordered the chassis for expensive cars like this and then went to a coachbuilder to tailor a body precisely to your tastes. The two most evenly matched competitors were Saoutchik and Figoni et Falaschi. They even "borrowed" inspiration from each other. Perhaps the only flaw to this nearly perfect design is the large proboscis, inspired by a whale. That design trend was short lived. The "art deco" sobriquet applies because of the streamlining and the chrome embellishments, as ornate as any art deco jewelry of the time.

The car's original customer was Sir John Gaul, an extrovert English millionaire who lived in Paris who had another car also bodied by Saoutchik. He was enamored of Lockheed's Constellation aircraft and that was said to have influenced his insistence on the extreme streamlining of the bodywork. Once he had the car built, he showed it at various concours, winning awards at concours d'élégances in Paris, Monte-Carlo and San Remo. Back in those days, when you exhibited such a car, you also had a beautiful lady posing beside it, the fabric of her gown dyed in colors to match the car (maybe even with a French poodle also dyed to match the car).

But, truth be told, it was a turkey to drive, not to mention the Cotal pre-selector gearbox kept packing up. After Dors had milked every ounce of publicity out of the car, it was dumped and she went on to a new Cadillac Eldorado convertible in 1955.

MAKE THIS A RUNNING CAR

A U.S.-based collector named collector Arthur Rippey bought it next but restoration didn't start until it fell into the hands of William G. Parfet in Colorado in the 1970s. I use the word "restoration" loosely because, after having a little too much trouble keeping it running, he sent it to the shop of Los Angeles based collector "Bud" Cohn and instructed him to put in a reliable drive train. This was, mind you, before Delahayes were considered valuable collector cars. So Cohn had the Delahaye six, the gearbox and the front suspension removed and slapped in a Oldsmobile Toronado 7-liter V8 mated to the front-wheel-drive transmission.

It was then sent to Pebble Beach in 1982, but even in those days Pebble was strict enough not allow such a cobbled car to compete for an award.

The car then went from one owner to another, each stymied by the fact Cohn had sold the mechanical parts on. Those who owned it but gave up on it were auctioneer Tom Barrett and later Sam Orenstein

Finally a Chicago restaurant owner who loved French built classics, bought the car all dismantled in 2003.

He got the car together. He sent it to the shop most qualified, Rod Jolley's coachbuilding firm in the New Forest in England, who had restored Bugattis and such. That firm put in more than 2000 hours of work. Some parts had to be made from scratch like the missing rear bumper.

It then went to a US restorer, Fran Roxas, to complete the restoration. By this time a spare engine and spare gearbox had been found and front suspension. The car was at last made complete and running. The restorers wanted to match the original paint, so they found some of the original under the bonnet.

After nearly three years' at Roxa's shop the completed car made its appearance at the 2006 Pebble Beach Concours. But alas it did not win Best of Show, the tendency at the time that a prewar car was the usual winner of that award. Giving a postwar car the top prize would upset the apple cart....

That was made up for the following spring, when it made its East Coast debut at the Amelia Island Concours, where it won the People's Choice trophy.

Lessons learned? Sometimes old cars kick around from one owner to another, in butchered condition, as this one did, for many years until their provenance is recognized and they get the restoration they well deserve. I am surprised that Barrett, co-founder of the Barrett-Jackson auction, didn't see this one through to the finish, but let's face it, some brands to Americans are more obscure than others and finding Delahaye parts probably discouraged him. The first time to buy it was when Dors tired of it. The second time was when it was still being shuffled around the country, all apart, still in boxes. Now that art deco French masterpieces are the stars of the fancier concours, you're not likely to find another "star" like this under a bushel basket but the same lesson applies to other marques—if your research determines a particular car is rare enough, it's worth buying and restoring.

What did it finally sell for, all spiffed up? At the RM Sothbys auction at Monterey in 2011, it rolled across the carpet and sold for around $3.3 million. They had predicted $4 to $6 million and I'm sure it would fetch that today.

Too bad Diana didn't live to see it. She died May 4, 1984, at the age of 52, from ovarian cancer.

Chapter 20
Sunset Strip Noir
(1950 Cadillac Fleetwood 60 Special)
Bulletproof Cadillac?
Hey, it made sense if you were a gangster....

Some things you don't forget. Mickey Cohen, in the wee small hours of the morning of July 20, 1949, couldn't forget pulling up to Sherry's Restaurant along Sunset Strip in West Hollywood with three buddies in his black 1949 Fleetwood 60 Special Cadillac, only to encounter a barrage of bullets. He and his companions escaped with only superficial wounds.

After being treated by some doctors, Mick decided his next car (a black 1950 Fleetwood 60 Special Cadillac) would have a little extra protection installed.

He took the new Caddy to a custom body shop in Hollywood and had it fitted with bulletproof glass an inch and a half thick. The windshield could be opened outward from the bottom; some say this was for shooting back at enemy attackers!

Who was Mickey Cohen, anyway? Meyer Harris Cohen was

a Brooklyn born kid who moved to the tough Boyle Heights are of Los Angeles with his family as a kid and became a small-time hood. He won the dubious distinction of being the most shot-at mobster in American criminal history since Chicago's George "Bugs" Moran. He boxed professionally, and when he ran that string out became a West Coast mobster in the 1940s and 1950s, starting out as "Bugsy" Siegel's bodyguard–a job he bungled, considering Siegel was rubbed out in Virginia Hill's Beverly Hills mansion. Some suspect it was because Meyer Lansky, a mobster instrumental in setting up casinos in Cuba, told Cohen to stay out of the way. So, Cohen's enemy was not Lansky, but Jack Dragna, the top mafioso in Los Angeles. The mob in those days took in their money from gambling, prostitution, narcotics and control of labor unions.

The turf war between Dragna and Cohen was sometimes referred to as the "Mickey Mouse war," because each time Dragna tried to stomp out Cohen, he failed. Twice, Cohen's home was bombed. One time, the bomb didn't go off. The other time just annoyed Cohen, as his collection of $300 suits got shredded).

A shotgun blast missed him, too, But the prize story is the time he was leaving a nightclub when, just as two hit men were pulling the triggers on their pistols, Cohen bent over to inspect a scratch on his Cadillac. The shooters missed. Eventually, Cohen was sent to the big house for five years on a tax rap. Years later, he was called before a congressional committee investigating organized crime where, Senator Charles Tobey asked, "Is it not a fact that you live extravagantly . . . surrounded by violence?" Cohen's answer? "Whadda ya mean, surrounded by violence? People are shooting at me."

Whatever you thought of him, he made good newspaper copy. For instance, when asked why a Hollywood banker made him a $35,000 loan without collateral, Mick's answer was, "I guess he just likes me." He also hung out with major movie stars like Sinatra, Dean Martin, and Robert Mitchum. He was a gangster, but a *likeable* gangster.

By the '70s, he was saying he would go straight, partly motivated by illness caused by a head injury he had received in prison. He died of natural causes in 1976.

BACK TO THE CAR

Oh, yes, the car. The shop he selected to do the work was Coachcraft in Hollywood, who had created customs for many a film star. Car collectors still argue whether Coachcraft's work should be classified as mere "customs" or deserve the more exalted adjective "coachbuilding," generally used with European coachbuilders, but regardless, all their work on Cohen's car was for naught because of a California law preventing a private party from owning an armored vehicle. The car had to be sold out of state. The car was later seen advertised in Tennessee. It now occupies pride of place in the Len Southward Museum, in Paraparaumu, NZ, along with Marlene Dietrich's 1935 V-16 town car. I'm sure the Museum visitors have heard of Dietrich, but when they see Mickey's car, it's probably "Mickey who?"

Chapter 21
The Search for the James Dean Speedster (1955 Porsche 356 Speedster)

When I was a kid back in the 50's, James Dean, an up-and-coming actor, was killed in a road accident when he was driving his race car to a race and I remember the local movie theatre in my home town, Berkley, Michigan, had a *"Tribute to James Dean."* I did not attend, being a little worried they would be showing the blood-spattered wreck, which I'd already seen pictured in the newspapers.

James Byron Dean was born February 8, 1931,and died while still in his twenties on September 30, 1955 while his most recent film was being edited. From what I can remember about his movies back then, he was sort of an instant icon.

He had made only three Hollywood movies by the time he died, first playing a loner in *East of Eden* (1955), which I have seen many times, trying to catch glimpses of Mendocino, where I spent part of my youth. Next was *Rebel Without a Cause.* Then came the role that cemented his sex appeal: Jett Rink, in *Giant* (1956), where Rock Hudson, the ranch owner, had to worry about his wife, played by Elizabeth Taylor, lusting after a ranch hand. Under normal circumstances, Dean would have been set up for many roles to come.

But here's the deal: he's got this film career racing forward full tilt boogie, but he's also a car racer, and, as a result of that ambition, he won the dubious distinction of being the first actor to receive a posthumous Academy Award nomination for best actor.

THE SPEEDSTER

His first Porsche was a glacier white, rear-engine Porsche 356 Speedster. He was killed in a mid-engined 550 which is also missing, leading to endless confusion.

The 356 hit the American market in 1952, after Max Hoff-

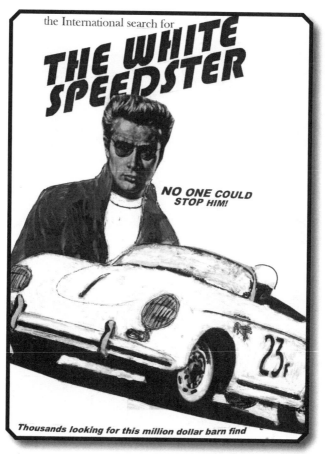

the International search for
THE WHITE SPEEDSTER

NO ONE COULD STOP HIM!

Thousands looking for this million dollar barn find

man, an Austrian importer operating out of New York City, figured out a lighter model, sans side glass, would sell, especially on the West Coast. His goal was to have a car that could be driven as transportation dring the week, and then on the weekend, you could dismount the glass windscreen and frame, put on a racing windscreen, and go racing. it looked sexier than the previous cars, because of its one-piece, low-cut curved windshield.

For an additional $500, enthusiasts could opt for the "Super" engine, which could propel the car up to 120 mph and sprint it from 0-to-60mph in about ten seconds. Before they introduced the mid-engine Type 550, the Speedster with the Super engine was Porsche's dual-purpose race car. Only about 154 Speedsters were equipped with that engine, then the four-cam Carrera engine arrived.

Automobiles of Arizona, in their 2009 auction catalog, listed a similar Super Speedster, saying "All told, about 4,000 Speedsters were assembled before production came to an end in 1959." Linking the car they had to the image of James Dean, they then wrote that, although it was a race car, "It also could, with little effort, even be enjoyed on the street and, as such, carries the dual Porsche pedigree embodied by such enthusiasts as James Dean himself."

His car-racing hobby began in 1954, reportedly in a Triumph Tiger T110. Just before filming *Rebel Without a Cause,* where the cars featured on screen were big ol' Mercurys, he ran races in Palm Springs on the last weekend of March, 1955, taking first place in the novice class, and second place in the main event. His racing career continued in Bakersfield a month later, where he finished first in his class and third overall. An Indiana boy at heart, he always told friends he yearned to compete in the Indy 500, and that film work interfered with his racing ambitions.

The white Speedster got hit on the right fender twice and the driver's door once. Dean always sent his car to the body shop after a crash, so he wouldn't have to explain the dents. Still, the crashes made the execs at Warner Brothers nervous, and he wasn't allowed to race during the production of *Giant.* Once he finished his scenes, though, he felt free to resume racing.

DEATH IN THE AFTERNOON

So, having done well in the 356, which was designed as mostly a road car, Dean upped the ante by buying a more serious, for-racing-only Porsche: a 550 Spyder (I know, some were street driven, but this was much more of a pure race car than the Speedster). Its first outing was to be a race in Salinas, California, on September 30, 1955. At the last minute before driving to the track, Dean stopped at George Barris's shop to have the words "Lil' Bastard" painted on the car.

Rather than trailer his race car, Dean wanted to do it the Euro way—drive the car to the track, race, then drive home with a trophy. In the car with him was Porsche factory mechanic Rolf

Wutherich, who had urged him to drive the car there to break in the engine. Following along in another car was stunt coordinator Bill Hickman (who you can see as one of the villains in Steve McQueen's film, *Bullitt*) and a *Collier's* magazine photographer, Sanford Roth. At 3:30 pm, both Dean and Hickman, who was following behind, were ticketed for speeding. I guess being a movie star don't cut no ice in the Central Valley.

As the group traveled Northward on U.S. Route 466, at approximately 5:15 pm, a1950 Ford Tudor, driven by a rube with the unlikely name of Donald Turnupseed, made a maneuver that brought him directly in front of Dean's speeding Porsche. Dean T-boned the driver's quadrant of the Ford Tudor. Turnupseed, with only minor injuries, sprang out of his damaged car to see what had happened to the occupants of the Porsche. Wutherich survived, having been thrown free from the severely mangled Porsche, but Dean died at the wheel, a broken neck among his injuries.

There have been numerous stories and even a book or two about the 550 Spyder's fate. I think it even toured around state fairs, where you could pay a fee to see the crumpled wreck. Then there's the story that it disappeared when it was being shipped by train. Every ten years or so I hear rumors it's been found. Or that parts from it were used in other Porsches and those cars crashed. I am not interested in what happened to that car—it's chasing too many ghosts, andI try to avoid writing about cars that people were killed in, as I find it all rather ghoulish.

As one very cruel writer wrote on a forum about Porsches vis a vis the whole James Dean story with cars: "There really isn't that much to the story. Flash-in-the-pan movie heartthrob driving a lightly built European sports car gets left-turned by a massive American car and becomes a legend. Best thing that ever happened to him career-wise, except for the dying part."

Forget the Spyder, What About the Speedster?

I am here not to be just another journalist getting on the deeply-rutted trail of the 550 Spyder, but to ask about the fate of Dean's *previous* Porsche, the 1954 Super Speedster, white in color.

I think the car's still out there, waiting to be found.

Due to the lingering interest in James Dean, I think it would have a phenomenal value at auction. A Ferrari 250GT Lusso ordered new by Steve McQueen recently fetched much more than the auction company's estimates. There's just something about pulling up to an outdoor café in an old sports car and, if someone asks, "Who did that belong to?" being able to drop a name like Steve McQueen or James Dean.

It is a matter of record that Dean traded the 356 in on the 550 Spyder. The dealer no doubt put the white Speedster out on the lot. The first thing any barn finder has to do is get a serial number.

Automobiles of Arizona, an auction company, selling a similar car in 2009, said that the James Dean Speedster was a 1955 Type 540 Super, serial numbered 80126. But a site called thesamba.com says it's 82621. So there you have it, Speedster fans, two places to start.

Adding fuel to the fire, if you go to a site called forum. porsche356registry.org on Jan. 27, 2011 a man named John Summer posted a message about his research saying "as the owner of two Speedsters, I was curious about what happened to Dean's white Speedster. Researching all available info, and with a friend in Germany who had access to the factory data base (cardex's, etc) I was able to narrow down the VIN number of Dean's Speedster to just one car. With the known combination of characteristics (colors, engine, etc) and the only potential delivery period from the factory to Competition Motors, where Dean purchased it perhaps less than two weeks after its delivery… #80126 with 3-piece Super Engine #41014 was the only possible car Dean could have bought. I kept this information to myself and my friend in Germany, hoping to locate the car."

Now I checked with a site called www.my356Speedster.com and they do list a Speedster having been made with the SN 80126. But the site is enigmatic. It has no place for comments like "And by the way this is James Dean's car." But they do say where this car is registered—France. Here is their actual listing, line for line:

```
80126.my356speedster.com // FRANCE
Chassis number:              80126
Model:                       Pre A
Year being built:            1954
Engine model:                1500S
Engine:                      41014
Horsepower @ RPM:
Drive position:              Left hand drive
Car color:                   Glacier White
Upholstery color:            Black with white piping
Carpet color:                Brown
Top color:                   Black
Mileage / KMs:               89,000 miles
Restored:                    Yes, The car is restored and numbers
matching
Condition:                   Undergoing restoration
Standard options:            Sealed beam headlights. US speedometer.
Remarks (opinion and modifications):
```

As to the confusion of model year, the car might have been made in 1954, but registered in California as a 1955 model, hence the confusion in model year from one website to another).

My appetite for finding this car increased by accident. Now, it so happens, in 2015, while in a hands-across-the-water mood, I had written a story on James Dean's Speedster and sent it to a 356 Club in France and other clubs around the world, thinking if I do something for them maybe they'll send something my way sometime soon. Damned if they didn't write me back and said "Oh, by the way, one of our members owns that car."

I was dumbfounded, because, I thought "How could this be when I saw that some ultra-fanatics in the U.S. had been looking for it for 40 plus years?"

I queried more but, by press time, didn't get a letter from the owner stating his proof or documentation for this claim.

Now if I were hired to "vet" the car prior to making an offer, what I would do is go there with a flashlight and, armed with information on the car's minor crashes back in the day, look at the inside of the relevant body panels to see where there is crash damage perhaps repaired with the "Bondo" of the era. Since these races were over 60 years ago, you'd have to find someone in the U.S. who had been at those races, someone with a good memory to confirm "Yup, it was that fender, etc." Or a known fact is that the chrome letters "Speedster" are known to have been removed by Dean, but it's possible they were put back on by a later owner but in a different location, so there would be four holes underneath, not two. But the only way to really tell if it's the Dean car is to try to get a list of owners from the last known owner in California –which I have heard was Lew Bracker, Dean's one-time room-mate, who bought it from the dealer after Dean traded it in on his race car—and all the previous owners the Frenchman can remember. If those two lists "meet" with one name in common, you got a winner.

OK, let's say the French owner backs off, and all claims of his car being the Dean car are off. I can live with that. Then I notice a picture on a website of that same car racing in France in recent events. The car has a number on the side. The number '23". Hey, nostalgia buffs, I ask you what number did Dean paint on the car when he raced it? "23."

There's a cosmic joke here somewhere, someone's having fun with someone but the lesson here for barn-finders is that celebrity cars are sometimes worth a lot more than the exact same car would be if its owner history only included a retinue of faceless Joe Schmos. I can just see someone like Brad Pitt toodling up to the Oscars in this car and, when the interviewer asks "Oh, that's such a cute car-- where did you get that?" and he casually drops the line: "Oh, that, it's James Dean's car," then it would be worth every penny of what he paid for it. Oh, some say you can't buy image but I assure you that you can, if the car was owned by the right guy…

I know, I know, why bother to look for a needle in a haystack? Because this particular needle is solid gold, my friends. Solid gold.

Chapter 22
The Corvette from Wisconsin—Via Italy
(1958-'59 Corvette)

OK, it's red and has a long hood and a short tail (a fastback) and it's bodied in Italy, so it's got to be a Ferrari right?

Ah, no.

It's called the Kelly Corvette. Based on a '59 or '60 Corvette (some reports even say 1961), I remember seeing it on the newsstand on the cover of *Car & Driver.* I remember envying Gordon Kelly for having the chutzpah (and the cash) to go to Italy to have a proper coachbuilder (Vignale) build his dream car on a Corvette chassis.

And then, wouldn'cha know, he has the brass to show it at the 1961 Paris Salon de l'Automobile on the Vignale stand.

The car has a modern look with its domineering egg-crate grille and nice fastback. One odd looking element are the chunky rubber bumper blocks in the back, but those actually hide the leaf springs for this solid-axle car (and I think Porsche stole the shape for the 928 bumpers decades later).

I finally saw the car in person a half century after it was built

at the Art Center College of Design's annual car show in Pasadena. It was everything I expected from the front and side, but looked a little too stubby from the back. And the interior wasn't Italianized enough for me, snob that I am.

When I saw it in person, it had eight-lug Pontiac wheels like the ones that used to be offered on the Pontiac Grand Prix in 1962. They looked great, but it confused me as to what the wheels were when this car first appeared.

I don't know if Kelly studied at Art Center, but I know he was an industrial designer and worked for Brooks Stevens in Wisconsin, who was a consultant on many American car designs and is remembered for the Excalibur. Maybe Kelly's designs were not much appreciated by his boss, so he did this one on his own, as if to say, "See what I can do, boss?"

I have no information on whether this grandiose exercise in self promotion propelled Kelly's career forward or not, but you have to admit that, more than a half century later, it puts his name on the list of American car designers, albeit a "one-hit wonder" as they say in recording circles. Wonder why Harley Earl or Bill Mitchell didn't call him up?

Apparently, Kelly only tried to sell the car once. I can't find the source, but there's a story that it was advertised for $8,900 in the Boston *Globe* until a magazine editor talked him out of selling it. It was only sold after his death by the estate.

Incidentally, Mr. Kelly said he had $13,000 in the car, which figures out right, with about $3,000 for the new car, $1,000 shipping and the rest for design and fabrication in Italy. It appeared at Pebble Beach in 1994 and at the Amelia Island concours about a decade ago, so it's been out and about the concours trail, but is almost a complete mystery car, one of those why-didn't-Detroit-notice-him kind of things.

Whoever owns it now published a nifty little book on it, very tasteful, which they handed out when it was at the Art Center show but, as usual, they leave out what they bought it for.

Now the question for the barn finder is: is this car significant historically? I say yes, because it was built by an Italian carrozzeeria that was at the top of its game around then (things went downhill after that, especially after DeTomaso bought them out and used them to build Panteras, which still wore "Ghia" badges, a slap in the face to Vignale because DeTomaso's patrons at Ford thought that name had more name recognition than "Vignale.")

But is it worth as much as, say, the Corvette Rondine, a 1963 Corvette coupe built by a rival frim, Pininfarina? And if not, why not? Well, I'd say part of the provenance (a word that means how "proven" or documented a work of art or antique is) of the Rondine is that Tom Tjaarda designed it, and Tjaarda designed at least two Ferraris—the 365 California Spyder and the much more common 330GT 2-plus-2. Plus, he is better known in Ford circles for doing the Pantera for Ghia. So there you have it, one guy, Kelly, is a flash-in-the-pan car designer with only one known car to carry his name, while Tjaarda (pronounced JAR-DUH) is a world famous designer, who has been in the field for well over 50 years.

So, lesson learned? An oddball one-off car can be exciting, but you have to explore its provenance before you whip out your checkbook. Who built it? Why was it built? Where did it appear in its original incarnation? If this car were cheap enough, and all you want is a car that gets attention, then you could justify it, but if it's terribly obscure, to be an astute barn finder, you can't budget an unrecoverable amount.

CHAPTER 23
THE MOTEL FIAT
(1953 Fiat 8V)

Coachwork by Vignale, a rare engine. It only took ten years to buy it...

When they say of a guy "he's got the eye" they usually mean the eye that can spot a beautiful woman in a crowd, the best house on the block to buy and the like. Well, there's also a case of having a good eye to spot a valuable car, even if it has fallen upon hard times and looks more than a bit rough around the edges. That's what happened to a Calif. guy who was just goin' fishin' and happened upon a diamond in the rough, a Fiat 8V.

First of all, the car, Fiats are largely mass-produced cars now but back in the Fifties, there was some special models that had artful bodywork that made them every bit the rival of Ferrari stylistically. One such car was the 8V premiered in Geneva in 1952. It was called the 8V" because Fiat had the mistaken impression that Ford owned the name "V8" so twisted it around so they could call their V8 "8V."

The tiny 1,996cc V-8 engine was exclusive to that car, and only 114 were built; most with a factory coachwork designed by Rapi, while a few were bodied by outside panelbeaters like Ghia, Siata and Vignale.

What makes this story a charming example of barn finding is that the barn finder was a man named Dan Simpson who was not even looking for a barn find when he first spotted the car. No sir, fact was he was going fishing up in the mountains in California and not thinking of cars at all when he first spied the car in a parking lot.

When he passed the car, he didn't notice exactly what car it was, he just knew it was Italian. Curiosity overcame him and he stopped and looked at the car. When he saw the Vignale coach-builder's badge, he began to realize he had discovered gold. The car's styling was vaguely like a Ferrari done by Vignale, maybe a 375, thought the car was smaller, sort of a 4/5ths scale Ferrari as it were (with 2/3rds the number of cylinders).

Now Simpson already owned a '52 MG TD, so he knew sports cars. But he knew by the sensuous coachwork that this one was in another realm, more hand built, probably cost twice the price of an MG when it was new. He went into the office and met a man named Shelly Pfeiffer, the hotel owner, who told him how he had acquired it.

Pfeiffer had actually acquired it years earlier, back when he was an aerospace engineer down in the South Bay. He and his wife were skiers and among the ski instructors was an Italian named Pino Lella. Pino was no ordinary ski instructor, he had actually been on the Italian Olympic ski team of 1950 and when the other Italian Olympians went home, he stayed. Though at that time you couldn't make much money as a ski instructor so he began importing sports cars, one at a time from Italy. He knew the foremost dealer in Milan, Gastone Cripaldi.

Now back to Shelly. He decided he wanted a Ferrari and asked his new friend if he could get one but Pino told him he could get a car that looked like one at a lower price so in '58, the 8V was bought from Cripaldi and shipped to Los Angeles. Shelly loved the car and was completely unaware that, in a former life, the car had run the 1955 Mille Miglia, driven by Mario Bonacina under the flag of Scuderia Madunina of Milano. It retired, alas before the end of the race but no matter, this was to be an important part of the car's resume.

Engineer owners are wont to save parts in case anything breaks and Shelly began salting away parts, sourced from local sources like Ernie McAfee, Hoffman Motors and Bill Rudd. But alas, once he put the parts together and started the car up, the crank broke as a result of improper heat treating, and, faced with a complete rebuild, he did what Yankee engineers sometimes do--he stuffed in an American engine.

In this case it was a Chevy II four cylinder, with the original engine traded to Alan Johnston, a friend and fellow worker at TRW, who also owned Siatas and 8Vs and had the confidence to rebuild the Fiat engine, which he intended to use in his own cars.

Well, when retirement loomed, Shelly moved to the mountains and Alan moved as well when he left TRW and, wherever he went, he had the 8V engine with him.

THE TEN YEAR SCHMOOZE

Now I never met Dan Simpson, the barn finder, but as a result of hearing this story about what followed after he found the car, I know he would qualify as a world class Schmoozer. That's the ability to turn somebody who's recalcitrant into thinking your way. For ten years after he first stopped and looked at it, he would stop at the motel every time he passed through town and shoot the breeze with Shelly, building a case for why he was qualified to own the car. By the fall of 1981, he finally wore down Shelly's resistance and bought the car. There was no argument about the price.

When he got home he researched the car more and found out that the designer was Michelotti while Vignale had done the coachwork. The car had been on show at the 1955 Turin Auto Salon labeled as a "Tipo Mille Miglia '55 Fiat 8V.".

The SN is 106000066. The car was made originally with engine 0136, and first sold in late December '54. When a *Hemmings* editor wrote about it, he didn't say what Simpson bought it for. But one person on an internet forum guessed the price back then, without an engine, would probably have been $3,000 which sounds fair to me since probably none had been imported new to America so it was basically an unknown commodity.

FINDING THE ENGINE

Simpson tried to think of a more Italian engine he could install, toying with the idea of a Fiat/Dino V6. As he wrote sources inquiring about Italian engines, he contacted John de Boer, an expert on oddball small displacement Italian cars, and Simpson began running an ad through de Boer to search for an 8V engine. But he was discouraged by the costs--far more than he had anticipated. But then he had a bright idea—why not find the man who had traded the engine from Shelly?

You have to understand, that this was in the pre-Google era, so it took real legwork. But he found Alan Johnston in Dallas, Texas, and contacted him. The good news was that Johnston still had the original engine and he had put it in his own Zagato 8V. But the bad news was that he was not interested in selling it. But he did hold out the offer that he would call Simpson first if he decided to sell it because he knew the significance of having an original engine in an original chassis.

Long story short, thirteen long years go by, the call comes from Texas. The engine is for sale. It was dismantled but intact, so the Simpsons bought it and it was put together and put in the car.

Where the car went from there, I am not too sure of. One report from Concorso in 2011 said Dan didn't restore it, though he did get it running. Another story said he was intent on selling it, to pay for the college education of four youngsters. But the lesson is there for car finders to learn from—if you are a connoisseur, you will always recognize a car with purebred DNA, even if it's in a molderin' away in a motel parking lot. .

Kudos to Simpson for sticking to his guns and buying the car with the non-original engine but still trying to get the original engine. When he re-united the two he probably improved the car's value ten fold (Maybe far more, as Gooding was estimating a restored version of the same model--one only a few serial numbers away from the Simpson car--would bring over $1.6 million at their Amelia Island auction in 2016).

I personally want to give Simpson kudos too, for showing the car unrestored. I am tired of cars that are restored with the wrong color ("well, the painter assured me that it was a close match") or the wrong upholstery, so one might well leave it as a mechanically restored barn find that runs and drives and show it that way, patina and all...

The only downside to this story is that it all took 23 years, a good chunk of a man's lifetime, to get the car into running form, meaning that was many, many events he missed, many Montereys and other events. I might have chosen a less rare car so I could enjoy it on the road during all those years. But the basic lesson is there— you're a connoisseur, so you can't let that jewel sporting a coachbuilder's badge get away, right?

Chapter 24
Brother from Another Mother
(1959 Ferrari 400 Superamerica)

Wherein a Fiat executive orders one coachbuild-er to build identical cars on rival firm's chassis...

We journalists often prefer to peg a car with the moniker of someone famous who owned it. Well, this one-off, 1959 Ferrari 400 Superamerica Coupe Speciale was owned not just by Giovanni Agnelli, the Chairman of Fiat, but also by Anita Ekberg.

Now I remember Ekberg. She was one of the first blonde bombshells from Sweden that made us Yanks realize Sweden was a place to keep on radar. One of her first films was the classic *Abbott and Costello Go to Mars*, which doesn't get played as much by film buffs as it should. Later, she was in a much more significant film, *War and Peace*. She romanced all the leading studly stars of the time, including Frank Sinatra, Tyrone Power, Yul Brynner, Rod Taylor, and Errol Flynn, and she was one of the first actresses to appear in *Playboy*.

Little did I know Ekberg liked Ferraris. And Italy. In fact, she

was in a Fellini film, *La Dolce Vita*, one of my favorites about the good life in Rome in the '50s.

The odd part about this car is that it doesn't look like you'd expect a Ferrari to look, and it certainly doesn't look anything like the later 400 Superamerica Aerodinamicos, which had pointy front ends with elliptical grille cavities and pointy back ends. This one is boxy by comparison. Because of the cut of the wraparound windscreen, it looks, as one reporter said, "like the whole thing is leaning forward, itching to grab a gear and go."

This car was bought new by Gianni Agnelli who, at the time, was chairman of Fiat (the company his family founded). The 400 Superamerica was the successor to the earlier 410 Superamerica. It was powered by a 4.0-liter V-12 rated at 340 horsepower. This was the first one built.

The car was redone between its first auto show appearance and its second one, little details like changing the front bumpers and cladding the lower half of the body in stainless steel. I had the opportunity to inspect this car firsthand at a car show in Pasadena and am amazed at how closely the steel is clad with the stainless (and wondering if there's a chance for rust to develop in between). Stainless is one of my favorite metals, so I'm interested in any car using it.

Agnelli sold it in 1962. At some point, Ekberg owned it. A Florida owner bought it sometime later and crashed it. It may have been sold as a wreck for as little as $11,000, at least it was advertised for that. Finally, when an owner couldn't sell it (and who would have replacement body panels for a one-off car?), it was donated to the Harrah's collection in the early 1980s, then restored.

It has changed hands since.

A Doppelganger

Only 47 Ferrari 400 Superamericas were built, and this car has the double distinction of being the first one built and the only one built with this styling. Ironically the car has a Doppelganger—it is not the only car with that exact same body styling.

Giovanni Agnelli also ordered a Maserati 5000 GT with almost the same body. He had Pininfarina body the Maserati (AM-103-008) with sheet metal almost identical to his Ferrari 400 Superamerica, commissioned from the same firm few months before.

That car didn't look like any of the other Maserati 5000 GTs either. Was this a contest to see which firm could build the most satisfying car with the same body? Did he own them both at the same time? This  was, mind you, well before Fiat bought Ferrari. Maybe. Looking back, there was a motive for this.

Maybe Giovanni was staging a little contest—which firm could build the better car using the same body style? The Maserati has a much less common engine, derived from a 450S race car engine. So, technically, the Maserati is the more rare of the two mechanically, though it's a tough comparison. Only 32 5000 GTs were made from '50 to '65.

The Ferrari came up at the Gooding auction at Pebble Beach in 2013, with the prediction it should go for $3,750,000-$4,500,000, but it was a no-sale. Methinks what they needed to move it off the red carpet and into the hands of a buyer was a lifesize picture of Anita Ekberg in her prime.

Lesson learned? In your searches, you will come across oddball cars here and there that don't fit your preconceived conception of what a certain marque should look like. In the Maserati field, it was the 5000 GT with this body style. Likewise in the Ferrari field, it was the 400SA with this same body style. The point is that both cars are revered now as great cars that have "one-off" status within their marques. So what if they're ugly? Embrace ugly. It's lots cheaper than pretty and, once the provenance is known, you could still end up a winner.

Chapter 25
The O'Shea Mercedes 300SLS Roadsters
(1957 Mercedes 300SLS)

Briefly race champions, are they out there somewhere?

Going way back, to the mid-'50s, there was a dentist, Paul O'Shea, in the U.S., who was an amateur race driver. He cajoled Mercedes into providing him a 300SL gullwing, with which he won several local races.

But on a visit to the factory, he saw the prototype 300SL roadster, a car not yet in production, and asked to be provided one of those for racing.

Mercedes realized that this was a good opportunity for them, as they wanted to get the roadster established quickly as they were phasing out the famed gullwing coupe coupe. But they were a little worried that the roadster was a bit heavy, heavier than the coupe. And all the roadsters were going to be steel-bodied (where 29 of the previous gullwing coupes had been all aluminum bodied) . They wanted to create the impression that the roadster was as zingy as the coupe, so they decided to provide one to American racers.

It would have an all-aluminum body.

O'Shea along with George Tilp, competed in the S.C.C.A. (Sports Car Club of America) series against Porsche, Jaguar, Aston Martin and Corvettes. But the SCCA didn't approve of the aluminum-bodied one as a production sports car so he had to race in D class against prototypes. He still won two . S.C.C.A. Championships in the car.

Sometimes the cars are called "SLS" which can be interpreted as "Sports Light Special."

The SLS followed much of the production car lines, except for a few variations. It had exhaust pipes exiting from (one or both?) side(s) and the "full bubble" European headlamps. The passenger side was blocked off with a metal tonneau cover. There was a Mercedes 300SLR style headrest fairing. There was no glass windscreen, instead a small plexiglass one similar to the racing 300SLR that had won the Mille Miglia. There was a scoop ahead of the small windscreen to bring in outside air to the passenger compartment. The wheels seem to be a mystery. In some pictures you see wheels bolted on with lug nuts and in other pictures you see a knock-off Rudge type wheel.In one article in a German magazine, they mention the possibility that Mercedes used aluminum chassis instead of the tubular bar space frame of steel. The same reference says they saved 5.3 kg through use of aluminum brake cylinders and the engine had an aluminum block and aluminum heads resulting in a power-plant that weighed 61 kg less than the production car. Since the races were short, they didn't need a full size radiator so that was cut in half.

When they were finished cutting weight the SLS racers were 337 kg lighter than a conventional SL and without fuel weighed in at under 920 kg.

TWINS

Note I refer to these long lost treasures in the plural. This is because it is thought now, a full half century later, that Mercedes attempted to pull a bit of a fast one on those dummy Americans.

They first sent over one car and that was the one seen and raced, but then, after a heavy smash-up, it was sent to Tilp's factory, where he had a racing shop, and emerged to race only a week or so later at another event. Everyone who knows race cars knows you can't rebuild a car like that after a wreck like that, so it became apparent that there were two. They didn't have to worry about being kicked out of the production class with the second car as it was already running as a prototype. It is thought the second car had aluminum only in the doors, bonnet and boot.

After O'Shea and Tilp won the '57 championship the two cars were shipped back to Mercedes HQ in the U.S. in South Bend, Indiana. Mercedes had at that time believed Studebaker was a good company to partner with in bringing cars to the U.S. (or they may have feared that, in tying in with the Big Three, they would be swallowed up...) They didn't realize Studebaker was a dying company, and eventually separated from them. Studebaker moved operations to Canada in 1964.

This author has seen pictures in *Automobile Quarterly* of the abandoned Studebaker factory with various Studebaker prototypes rusting away. Perhaps the two Mercedes SLS roadsters were in there as well? Maybe the photographer didn't care about Mercedes and thus didn't bother to shoot them?

But they could have been sold. A German article writer said that Mercedes sold both of them after the racing season, one for $5,000 the other for a similar amount. One wonders why, if the SN are known, why nobody in the GullWingGroup or 300SL clubs has popped up with the cars in the last 60 years? O'Shea died in 1991, apparently never to find out what happened to "his" cars.

And so it remains. If either can be found and restored to their '57 racing trim they would be valued at a million-dollars each if worth a dime. How could they so totally disappear?

What serial number should you look for if perchance to run across one of the two? Hajo Lutke in an article on the German language website *mb300sl.de* says they are 8467 198 106/2 and 8442 620 070/1.

One last theory is that the cars had either magnesium body-work or magnesium chassis or both. Magnesium is lighter than aluminum. But it has one property you don't like to think about. It is the only metal that burns. The track officials at Le-Mans in '55, when a Mercedes 300SLR went into the stands and caught fire discovered that. Over 80 spectators were killed. They couldn't put the fire out. So to admit that only two years later they were fielding magnesium bodied cars in American racing would have been a no-no. I have no proof but if and when the cars are found, the truth will out....

Chapter 26
The Socialite, the Ferrari and the Grave That Holds Them Both (1964 Ferrari 330GT)
Wherein I draw the line as to how far I'll go...

I think, being a barn finder, you have to draw the line somewhere, like not calling a family to see if they want to sell the old man's Ferrari before the deceased's body is even cold.

But this is a case where the deceased has been deceased for some decades. By now, the more recent heirs might be amenable to a change in the status of the interred, if only to remove from the public's collective memory a controversial burial that involved a lady who loved life and her blue Ferrari.

The lady in question lies in a historic cemetery in San Antonio's Eastside; not in a normal grave, but in a custom-built box containing both her and her Ferrari.

She was Sandra Ilene West, a wealthy Beverly Hills socialite who died at age 37 (some say 38). She came by her money by

marrying right. Her husband was Ike West, Jr., the scion of one of the first families of Texas. I picture, in my mind's eye, the family in the TV series *Dallas*. Like that.

The original West brothers (George, Ike, Sr., and Sol) made their fortune as cattlemen running cattle drives in the 19th Century. When oil came along in the 20th century, they invested and hit it big in the 1920s and 1930s. By the time Sandra came along, the urge to break out of the family mold struck Ike, Jr., so he and Sandra moved to southern California in 1963. Ike became a securities trader and Sandra a new superstar on the Beverly Hills social scene. Add a Beverly Hills Mansion, flashy clothes, fast cars, celebrity boyfriends, the whole nine yards.

Oh, I'd be remiss if I didn't mention that Ike, Jr., didn't make it for the whole ride. He was a drug user and had rapid weight fluctuation. He died under clouded circumstances at the Las Vegas Flamingo Hotel in 1968, making Sandra a Beverly Hills socialite *and* monied widow. As such, she sort of lived up to a "Texas rodeo queen" image, with furs, rhinestones, bright well-fitted clothing, and stylish hats. Her fleet of bolides included a Stutz Blackhawk and at least three Ferraris: a 330 America, a 1969 365GT 2+2, and a 1973 Dino.

The accident, while driving her 330GT, happened in 1977. That didn't make the headlines but her burial the same year did, as her will insisted that she be interred sitting in the driver's seat of her favorite car, clothed in an elegant, white nightgown.

There was some disagreement among Ferraristi as to exactly *what* model it was that she was interred with. If you look hard enough on the net, you'll find a picture of her sitting on the hood of not a Lusso, as has been reported, but a more ordinary 330GT single-headlight model. It was also described as a "third series 250GTE with a 330 engine." Fifty were built. Her car is listed in the 330GT Register as SN 5055, a 330 America imported to the U.S. by Luigi Chinetti Motors, Inc., who it sold to West.

Which makes it a "one-owner" car, an important criterion in the collecting world.

By the way there's a rumor that she also had a 1972 365 GTB/4 Daytona Spyder, a car with considerably more panache and value. (I know, I know, the Daytona Spyder is supposed to be called a 365GTS/4, but some experts say there was a difference in numbering between the U.S. and the European models). And there is still, decades later, the contention that *this* was the Daytona she wanted to be buried in, but that someone instead substituted the 330GT in which she had crashed.

After she died, there was a holdup in carrying out her wishes because there was the problem of three wills being found, each with different heirs. A legal battle between her brother-in-law, named an heir in one will, and her lawyer, followed. It wasn't until April, 1977, that the wishes of Ms. West's 1972 will were granted by a court ruling. The court decided, by the way, not to fix the Ferrari and instead directed it be placed in a box with her behind the wheel as per her instructions.

The funeral, which cost $15,000, had its Hollywood aspects. Jack Palance, a star of many a cowboy movie, gave the eulogy and then, under the glare of television lights and with over 150 spectators in attendance, the box containing Ms. West (dressed as per her instructions, though accounts differ as to whether it was a negligee or a lace nightgown) seated inside her beloved Ferrari 330 America was lowered into a 20-foot-long grave. Her will asked that she be positioned "with the seat slanted comfortably."

Her grave at the Alamo Masonic Cemetery at 800 Center Street in San Antonio lies with that of Ike West, Jr. Visitors hoping to see some monument to Ferrari see only a slab of stone laying flush on the grass bearing her name and birth and death dates.

Once she was buried, debate ceased on lingering questions about her death.

Her decision to be buried with a Ferrari, though, had not been sudden. She had written that into her will four years prior to her death.

As to how collectable this Ferrari is, I would put it far behind the rumored Daytona Spyder (if indeed it can be established that she ever owned one) or the other two Ferraris. Plus, there is a rumor that the engine had to be taken out of the Ferrari "for environmental reasons." It would be worth much less without an engine. So, as a barn finder, I have to draw the line somewhere and say you won't see me picking up the phone and calling the heirs. Maybe if it were a Lusso, or Daytona Spyder...

Chapter 27
Master Builder, So-So Designer
(1970 Cadillac NART Zagato)
Some of the right team...but only some

Okay, let's say it's the early '70s and we were going to assemble an all-star team to develop a really swoopy, bodied-in-Italy sedan.

For the coachbuilder, we'd pick Zagato who, because of cars like the Alfa GTZ Canguro, is revered. For the drivetrain, uh, I'm afraid that's where this trolley goes off the track-nothing Italian here, but some big, old cast-iron hunk from a Cadillac Eldorado, mated to a TurboHydramatic. Since the Eldo at that time was front drive, we switch it around to make it mid-engine. No big deal.

Now for the designer, well, here's where we get controversial: Luigi Chinetti, Jr., of the car distributorship NART (for North American Racing Team), which was started by his father to im-

port Ferraris to the U.S. Chinetti, Sr., was famous for winning LeMans, first as a driver, in '49, and then as a sponsor ('65, with a 250LM).

Well, it happened that around 1969 or so Chinetti Jr. was on a roll. He was having Ferraris re-bodied in Italy by Michelotti, a famous coachbuilder. He was designing the cars in America, but having them built in Italy.

He had friends at GM. Powerful friends. The rumor is that, when he thought up this four-seat sedan with the Eldo drive-train flipped around amidships, his buddies at GM made full-size clay models of his designs for the car, which he said would be bodied in Italy. Bill Mitchell was VP of GM back then, and if I know Mitchell (and I did, actually), he would have been all for it, given that he wanted so much Italian influence in the Oldsmobile Toronado that he even approved buying a Ferrari 330GT 2+2 and bringing it to the clay model studio to inspire his designers.

Well somewhere along the way, plans went awry. GM ran smack dab into some sort of trouble in '69—can't remember what, now, strikes or a downturn in the economy, maybe all the safety regulations. Anyway, they bowed out of the project. No time for it. But Luigi, Jr.? He soldiered on. Quitters never win and winners never quit, etc.

He gets it built. It looks sort of Italian but is monstrously big. The only American content seems to be Toronado-style wheels, though it has also been pictured with Italian mags.

The car made its debut at the 1971 Turin Auto Show at the Zagato booth. While at the New York International Automobile Show, it graced the Chinetti Motor's stand.

Lou, Jr., was standing by, ready to take orders, but by then Ferrari business was booming, and there was the problem of making cars which would meet the U.S. bumper standards. Lots of serious stuff to be dealt with or Ferrari could say bye-bye to the U.S. market.

So the NART Caddy got pushed to the back of the shop and plans to build a second car were cancelled.

There was a buyer for the car, however, a man named Melvin A. Olshansky of Glencoe, Illinois, who bought it seventeen years later. Mel was a big-time car collector, and chairman of the largest sporting goods company in the U.S. He also had owned at one time a Saoutchik bodied '48 Cad, so he was a man who could be seduced by Euro-bodied American iron. By the time he got the Zagato NART Cad, it had deteriorated and was taken to a restoration shop where, for two and a half years, it was restored by Mill Creek Motors and Upholstery Unlimited of Clinton, Iowa.

The NART Cad appeared at the 2006 RM Auction in Monterey where it was estimated it would sell for between $50,000 and $100,000.It sold for $57,750; a rumor says it was, in fact, bought back by the owner because the "no reserve" maximum bid was, in his opinion, inadequate.

It gets worse. The car was taken to Europe and offered for sale a couple of times on eBay. The highest bid was a mere $16,766. One wag, reporting this incident said, "Obviously, this car is not a 'keeper' but a 'seller.'"

Meanwhile, other NART re-bodies, admittedly those based on V-12 Ferraris like the Ferrari 3Z spyder and also bodied by Zagato, were fetching big dollars on the auction circuits. So there's a lesson in there somewhere, like, uh, even having a famous coachbuilder doesn't guarantee you will get an appreciating result. Maybe Lou Chinetti should have had the Italians design it as well? Or how about, "You can put lipstick on a pig but it's still a pig?"

But there's a new twist. Well, not exactly new, as this tidbit goes back to a Cadillac club newsletter printed in April, 2009, where a Missouri man says he found a second and possibly a third NART Caddy by Zagato.

One critic's response to that news was to say that only a photo of two of them side by side would convince him there was more than one. But still a search for pictures on Google images done today comes up with a red one and a tobacco brown one, with the emblems different on each one (one says NART across the bonnet). But that could be the same car repainted. But then pictures show the two cars with two different color interiors, one light, the other black leather with red piping. The plot thickens.

And so it is. A mystery Caddy. Or Caddies. Zagato is a great coachbuilder, though I'd put the NART Zagato Cad far, far behind some of their other achievements and maybe leave it out of any Zagato history book.

You have the conundrum of a world-class coachbuilder building a car on a drek chassis, to a design of some Italian-American in New York who really was trying to steer Italian design into new directions. He should have just let Zagato do its own thing, and maybe he'd have ended up with a more beautiful car.

And Lou Chinetti, Jr? He went on to create more cars, including a Ferrari Daytona station wagon (okay, "a shooting brake," though I'll be damned if any American ever called his station wagon a shooting brake...), a Ferrari race car restyled with a sedate gullwing body for the street, and other treasures. Don't worry if he made out, he rebodied the gullwing car with a race car body again—so it looked like it did when it ran at LeMans. If he's still got any of the mid-engine Ferraris that ran at LeMans at the back of the shop, they have to be worth, what, $10 million each?

Now, can I predict whoever takes the NART Zagato Cad to auction will also come out ahead? Well, let me say it ain't over 'til it's over...or until the last bidder leaves the tent.

Chapter 28
The Jewel in the Crown
(1957 Ferrari Testa Rossa)
Not for sale, but for trade. Who'da thunk?

Didja ever feel like hitting yourself in the head with a hammer because you missed an all-time great deal? Oh, sure, maybe I never had the moola to buy that Ferrari Testa Rossa I saw as a kid in the Henry Ford Museum in Dearborn, Michigan, but my excuse is that I didn't know it was for sale.

You see, back in those days, like most people, I had the mistaken impression that all those cars that were out there on display were there forever; that, when they were donated, there must have been a stipulation in the donator's will that the car must remain there forever.

Not so. In almost all cases, there is fine print in the contract that says the museum has the right to do what they want with any donated car in order to meet their mission. In this case, the

misson of the Henry Ford Museum was to promote the genius of the first Henry Ford and secondly to promote the growth of American car history. When, out of left field, they received a 1957 Ferrari Testa Rossa race car from a man named Art True more than 30 years ago, it didn't really meet their mission. But what the hell, visitors to the museum enjoyed it, most being American car fans to whom seeing a pureblooded Italian racing car was a pleasant surprise.

Let me give you a fast look at this car's history. Chassis 0704 was one of two factory prototypes. The engine was a 2,953cc V-12. The first 250 Testa Rossa prototype, chassis 0666, used a 290 MM chassis, while the second prototype, number 0704, was built on a 500 TR chassis instead. Its race debut was at Le-Mans in 1957, where drivers Olivier Gendebien and Maurice Trintignant retired from the race early with a burned piston.

On the car's next outing, at the Grand Prix of Sweden, it again retired early, this time with gearbox problems. The car's first completed race came at the end of the 1957 season, when Phil Hill and Peter Collins drove 0704 to a fourth-place finish at the Grand Prix of Venezuela. The following season would open with a pair of wins at Buenos Aires and Sebring, with Hill and Collins again behind the wheel.

From there it went to American-based (but Austrian born immigrant) Johnny von Neumann, a racer who owned a Ferrari distributorship in California. He not only put Ritchie Ginther in it, but his stepdaughter, Josie, who raced in many West Coast events.

In 1960, it was in the hands of Jack Nethercutt, Jr., (who owns the magnificent Museum in Sylmar CA) and then went to Dick Hahn of Yakima, Washington, who had Jerry Grant as the driver in an incredible number of West Coast events. In '62, it went to Arthur True. By then, the car was getting rather long in the tooth, but had still been raced in "real" races (as opposed to vintage races, where the cars normally aren't driven as hard).

True raced it in vintage events in the Northwest, like the Seattle Seafair race, then, when he died in 1967, the car was donated to The Henry Ford Museum. It is an unusual race car, in that it never had a serious crash, making it one of the most original Ferrari 250 Testa Rossa models remaining where many have been crashed and rebuilt so many times their body shapes were only approximations of the originals.

THE TRADE

Fast forward some 30 years. A man named Jerry Helck, the son of Peter Helck, a famous fine-art painter of prewar race cars, put together a deal to trade the Ferrari for a classic American car, a Locomobile. Not just *any* Locomobile, mind you, but the most famous Locomobile race car ever: "Old 16," the car that won the 1908 Vanderbilt Cup, becoming the first American-made car to win that race. A car, historically, that is as important to American-made car auto racing history as, say, the *USS Missouri* is to U.S. naval history. The elder Helck had bought it in 1941.

It turned out Helck was not procuring the Testa Rossa for himself, but for a car dealer. Details are sketchy, because it was a private deal. Dragone Classic Cars, an American dealership, claims they were involved in the sale. How it was wangled out of the Ford museum is one of the great untold stories, but not all the facts have been disclosed. All that is known is that, in 1997, the Henry Ford Museum sold chassis 0704 to Helck and then the next owner listed is Abraham "Abba" Kogan, of Great Britain.

In 2004, the car moved on, various sources listing it as belonging to Eric Heerema, a Dutch car dealer in England. It was then restored by Neil Twyman, who drove it at the Festival of Speed in 2005, and a year later it was in a Phil Hill tribute parade there.

In April 2014, according to barchettacc.com, it was sold again via Damian Perl, UK to Tom Hartley, Jr.–who paid £24.1 million. Suffice to say the car keeps going up in value.

Back in Dearborn, the Museum got some flack for not realizing the value of the Ferrari. It was, as one wag described it when viewed looking back, "an unequal trade of monstrous proportions."

Upon selling the car, Hartley said of the Ferrari's significance, "This Ferrari is without question one of the most important cars on the planet, if not the most important, because of its originality. While I won't go into the terms of the sale, I am sure it will prove to be a great investment for the new owner."

Ferrari historian Marcel Massini said, "It is so valuable because it is totally unmolested and not restored, genuine and very original." Of course, the car has been kept in pristine condition, looking as alluring as the day it raced the 24 Hours of LeMans.

So, considering Helck beat us to it, is there still a lesson to be learned here? Yes, indeedy. And that lesson is: when cars are donated to museums, there is no rule carved in stone that they have to keep them forever, or even display them. The donor usually gets a nice tax write off, so they are happy with that, not insistent on controlling the car's future forevermore. Some car museums—such as the Petersen in Los Angeles—have three times as many cars in storage as they have on display. And you can bet many are unrestored or of less historical importance than their former owners thought, or inimical with the museum's mission statement.

So I say, when you go to a car museum, and you see a car you like, do a little background research to see what the museum's stated mission is, and what cars they are on the lookout for to better fulfill their mission. Maybe you can do a similar trade on a smaller scale—get them a car that more fulfills their mission and offer it in trade for a car that does not. And, more important, get a tour of the basement or upstairs floor of their parking structure or warehouse. Those are where the *real* treasures are.

Clue: you may have to volunteer at the museum to get such access, but, hey, I never said this would be easy...

Chapter 29
The Blue Goose
(1931 Mercedes 540K roadster)
Remember when one of the perqs of war was loot and pillage?

In the old days, back in the 1940s anyway, when US troops invaded an enemy country, there was not so much care taken to preserve the enemy's possessions. Hence, when the 101st Airborne rolled into a mountain area in search of Hitler and his henchman and spotted a unique, baby-blue Mercedes, they grabbed onto it as a prize of war.

But not before taking a shot at it to see if it was bulletproof, as it seemed to have unusually thick side glass and a bulletproof shield that could be raised behind the passenger compartment.

As they suspected, it turned out to be a high Nazi official's car, in this case Reichsmarshall Hermann Goering, who had fled the area earlier with several other cars jammed full of oil paintings and sculptures he was stealing.

THE 540K: ULTIMATE PREWAR MERCEDES

First a little background on the car. In the early '30s, Mercedes decided they had the capability of building the best luxury car in the world. The 500K became that, with its long hood and short tail; eventually the engine was bumped up to 5.4 liters, thus making the 540K. Only 25 Mercedes-Benz 540K Special Roadsters were ever made (some sources say 32); there would have been more but the war intervened.

It was launched at the 30th Salon de l'Automobile, in Paris.

Noted auto historian Griffith Borgeson described the Special Roadster: "There is a harmony and balance of line and mass... which very simply defies any conceivable improvement. They are sculptural perfection. For many people of taste, more beautiful cars will never be designed and built."

Hitler had ordered autobahns built in the late '30s, and this was just the car to cruise at 100 mph. The 540K's engine cranked out 115 bhp without the supercharger engaged, but soared to 180 bhp when the compressor kicked in. Top end was 110 mph.

THE GOERING CAR

In 1937, Reichsmarshall Hermann Goering ordered a 540K, eschewing the usual jet black paint job favored by other Nazi officials. No, his color of choice was sky blue, with his family crest on both doors. His nickname for the car was "The Blue Goose."

In May 4, 1945, it was all over for the Third Reich. The high brass was on the lam, trying to decide whether to let themselves be captured by the Americans or the Russians. That was the day the U.S. Army, C Company, 326th Engineers, 101st Airborne Division 'Screaming Eagles' entered Berchtesgaden, near Hitler's Eagles Nest, and found the car. Goering himself was captured three days later, in an entourage that was traveling in five more Mercedes.

As often happened, some high brass on the U.S. side commandeered the vehicle; thus, with 101st Airborne painted on the bumpers and a two-star license plate attached, was it used by Major General Maxwell Taylor until, back in D.C., they thought it could be used as an attraction at a war bond drive. So the car went to the US where, yes, indeed, it was schlepped around to sell bonds.

THE TIME TO BUY

Every collector car has an ideal time for a barn finder to buy it and, in this case, that time came almost 11 years later, in 1956, when the car was auctioned off by the US Army at the Aberdeen Proving Grounds in Maryland. The buyer was Jacques Tunick of Greenwich, Connecticut, with a high bid of $2,167. Seems cheap now, but back then a two-bedroom house in the 'burbs was maybe $11,000.

The car was no doubt Goering's car. It had to be adapted to hold him, the slim fighter pilot of WWI fame having ballooned to 220 pounds by the mid-1940's. Another tip-off it was his car was the left-hand, blue-lensed, spotlight.

Then a prominent collector of prewar Mercedes entered the picture: Dr. George E. Bitgood, Jr., a veterinarian. He probably bought it because he liked Mercedes, not because he was a fan of Goering, though, oddly, he had by sheer chance met Goering in Stockholm before the war when Goering was drinking with buddies at the bar.

Bitgood bought it in 1958 for a reported $10,000. Bitgood had started collecting the big classics during the war. The public didn't want them, because ordinary citizens were allowed only three gallons of gas per car, per week. Other notable cars he owned included Jack Warner's (of Warner Brothers Movie Studios) 1937 Mercedes Benz 540K Special Roadster and another 540K Special Roadster.

He eventually got as many as 14 of the big Mercedes; four were Special Roadsters. Showing no respect for provenance, Bitgood, for some reason, painted the Goering Special Roadster black, thereby obscuring the coat-of-arms painted on each door. Then, he had two brass plates fabricated with engraved swastikas and had each attached to a door. However, he did not have the bullet hole repaired in the fender, nor did he attempt to replace the damaged glass in the left driver's window with new bulletproof glass. Only once did Dr. Bitgood display the Goering Special Roadster.

Back in those days, your author remembers seeing a "Nazi staff car" at the Michigan State Fair. So it was common to show these cars, these "fortunes of war" back then. The Doctor had been hiding the cars from the public for years, then suddenly rolled it out in 1973 in Durham, Connecticut, for the Durham County Fair. For some reason, he thought it would be a money-maker and charged people two bits to see it.

After the Durham Fair, Bitgood contacted the 101st Airborne Division in Fort Campbell, Kentucky, offering to bring the Blue Goose to a reunion in 1974. That plan was cancelled when he was diagnosed with cancer, but it turned out his daughters were interested in honoring the 101st Airborne—who had originally captured the car—and wanted to fulfill their father's dream of reuniting the Blue Goose with the remaining veterans of World War II.

Bitgood's son-in-law prepared the car for the 101st Airborne Reunion at Fort Campbell, Kentucky, in June, 2002. The car was also shown at the Pebble Beach Concours d'Elegance.

Many collectors wanted to buy it and restore it, but Dr. Bitgood had wanted to restore it only as it looked when captured. So the heirs interviewed collectors until they found one from Sweden who promised to restore the 540K the way the doctor had wanted. Classic Auto Services, in Oxford, Maine, did the restoration.

Lesson learned? That war provides opportunities for collectors. Property changes hands big time. By the time of the Iraq war, though, apparently the US Army had changed its attitude, because I don't recall Saddam's cars (including a Mercedes 540K that he had stolen from an Iraqi museum) being brought to the U.S. for tours.

As for the Goering car, fans of pre-war Mercedes knew the U.S. government had it, so the smartest barn-finder was the guy who found it on the list of surplus property...and bought it for the price of a new Buick. Today, its value would be more along the lines of $25 million.

Chapter 30
The GTO that Wasn't a GTO - Temporarily (1962 Ferrari 250GTO)

The time to buy it was when nobody knew what it was....

Imagine a situation where a tipster calls you and says, "Hey I got a great Ferrari offered to me. It doesn't look like a 250GTO, but the seller swears six days to Sunday it is one underneath."

Uh-huh. Why not line up that bridge in Brooklyn at the same time?

Truth is, there was indeed a 250GTO that went without a GTO-shaped body for a few years. At which time it was probably offered for less than your regular production Scaglietti-bodied 250GTO.

Everybody and his brother knows about the 250GTO, the race car Enzo Ferrari ordered Giotto Bizzarrini to build after he had seen the Jaguar E-Type and feared his short-wheelbase 250GT wasn't aerodynamic enough to compete with the svelte cat from England.

So Giotto moved the engine back and down and added a dry sump and a 5-speed and a body that was more pointed at the front. He arrived at the GTO body shape by gooping the Italian version of Bondo onto his mule car and running it on the autostrada night after night, trying different shapes until he could get it up to 175 mph. Then that design was replicated in aluminum on a short-wheelbase chassis. No car designers needed here, thank you very much.

Everyone who likes real cars and model cars likes the Series I GTO shape with its fastback and little ducktail. Everyone except the designers at Pininfarina, who didn't like it because they didn't think of it, so they came out with the Series 2 body which borrows from the 250LM a lot and even has a "tunnel back/sugar scoop" 250LM roof. Some owners of Series I cars even went into the shop to get Pininfarina Series II coachwork. (Racers you find, have no respect for tradition and will throw out last year's body if the new one promises to be faster}

Let me go into the history of No. 3445.

Barchettacc.com, a website that specializes in Ferrari history, says that the first owner was Luciano Conti, in Bologna and the same year it wen to Sergio Bettoja in Rome. With Bettoja it recorded its first race coming in third in class. Then in '62 it went to The King, or technically , the Count

THE KING OF VENICE

He wasn't really a king, but the car's next owner had so much power in Venice, he was equivalent to a king. He was Count Giovanni Volpi, who ran a racing team called SSS (Scuderia Serenissima Repubblica di Venezia). It was the Count who put Vacarella and Scarlatti, two works Ferrari drivers, into the still stock-bodied GTO for the 1962 24 Hours of LeMans. They didn't win but they did come in first in the Nine Hours of Auvergne at Clearmont Ferrand the same year. You wonder how he got Ferrari team drivers, maybe it was as some suspect, that Volpi owned the car on paper but it was SEFAC Ferrari picking the drivers.

At any rate, it was finally sold by the Count and ended up in the hands of Swedish racing driver Ulf Norinder, who is believed to have campaigned it from 1963 through 1971. Among the venues he raced it at were the Targa Florio, Monza, Daytona, Spa, Nurburgring, Reims and any number of Swedish events. Again some believe it was all a behind-the-scenes effort directed by Ferrari, and it's indeed odd that Nordinder wasn't always the piloto; sometimes it was Jackie Stewart or Chris Amon. I think that fantasy of it being backed by Ferrari would only apply to its early years, maybe, but surely after '65, Enzo had bigger fish to fry...

THE SMASHUP AND THE AFTERMATH

The car got its mysterious body from another coachbuilder because it had a big smashup, one so bad that it was deemed better, i.e. less expensive at the time, to go with a new body by an outside metal bender than to ask Pininfarinato make a Series II body or Scaglietti to make a Series I. In truth, probably neither would want to because it was an old design by then.

With this new body it was sorta like a GTO–but different in almost every line, as if the GTO had a fraternal twin brother. A brother from another mother...so to speak.

The coachbuilder was a firm called Carrozzeria Sports Cars, which was a niche carrozzeria in Modena, a firm whose high point came in the 1960s. Reportedly its founder, Pierre Drogo, had at one time run in F1. When he started his shop, he specialized in repairing smashed race cars and sometimes building new bodies for them. His coachwork was seen on cars for by Scuderia Serenissima and Bizzarrini, and even some Ferraris sport his work, though it's doubtful any of those cars were commissioned by someone named Enzo.

In '71, Robert Lamplough, an Englishman, bought the car and raced it at events until 1976, when it had another big accident and was re-bodied as a Series I GTO, with the historically correct Scaglietti body style. He continued to race it at vintage events like the Ferrari 25th anniversary. In December, 1991, it was taken to the Poulain le Fur Paris auction, where the owner turned down $5,314,000.

It is then listed by *Barchettacc.com* as going to William Bauce, Rancho Santa Fe, California, and then being offered in May of '96 for $3,500,000 by SMC, La Jolla, California, a famous exotic car dealership. Then it went to Japan for five years to be part of the Matsuda collection, and has moved onward since. In '03, citing barchettacc.com again, it went to Charles Arnott of Maryland who traded three Ferraris for it, including a '550s model, a 212 Export, a 250LM and a modern race car, a 333SP. He had Symbolic Motor Cars' Bill Noon pilot it at three events and then himself took it to the Cavallino Classic in 2005.

The next owner was Christopher Nixon Cox of Chapel Hill, North Carolina, (if that middle name strikes a bell, yes, he *is* a grandson of the former President) who became temporarily infamous in vintage racing circles for putting the car through its third major shunt as he attended the 50th anniversary event of the Ferrari GTO in France. He was on a highway passing another car when it happened. The car had severe damage, and his wife broke her leg, but he was nonplussed. He later divorced that wife, who he had only been married to for a year when they had the accident. (Maybe she didn't like his driving.)

David Gooding, the auctioneer later told a newspaper that if was repaired correctly, it wouldn't hurt the value

THE TIME TO BUY

Lesson learned? One man's catastrophe could be another man's fortune. The absolute best time to buy this car was:

1. The day it was smashed with its original body.
2. The day it was smashed with its replacement body
3. The day it was smashed with its third body (the 250GTO style body)

A lot of potential buyers of Ferraris back when it had the Drogo body walked right by this car and didn't recognize its

142

DNA. At that time, books on the GTO hadn't yet been published, so I am sure a lot of people who saw the car and heard "that's a GTO underneath" said "Yeah, sure, and pigs can fly."

Now it's too late.

Today, any 250GTO is worth between $38 and $52 mlllion, the most recent selling prices this author has noted. And, hey, it's only 2016. At this rate of appreciation, they will be $100 million each by 2025

Chapter 31
The DiDia 150
(1961 Cadillac)

One big step for Bobby Darin, one small step for car design...

You might be wondering why there aren't custom cars in this book. Oh, there are cars that have been fettled with, made special for their owners, but I mean good ol' American-as-apple-pie customs like George Barris or Gene Winfield built.

This story is a case in point as to why not.

But I am still attracted to writing about the car. Okay, I, too, am tired of reading about past movie stars, like Steve McQueen and James Coburn, being praised for buying the right car way back when, cars that are worth millions today. But what if I told you about a popular crooner who had his own dream car built, from scratch almost. Where is the applause for him?

I speak of Bobby Darin, singer of one of my favorite songs, *Mack the Knife.*

Actually I was wrong when I said he ordered it built. That's in a lot of newspaper accounts, but the fact is he bought it as a used car from Andrew DiDia, a clothing designer, who Bobby Darin had met in Detroit while on tour in 1957. Darin told DiDia at the time that he would come back and buy the car if he ever "hit it big."

He did. Make it big. And bought the car.

It was not a cheap car to build. It was under construction for seven long years, from 1953 to 1960. Called the DiDia 150, it was hand-built by four workers at a cost of $93,647.29. At least DiDia made a profit—he sold it to Darin in 1961 for over $150,000 (1.5 million today).

That was such a huge price at the time that the car was listed as the most expensive "custom-made" car in the world by the *Guinness Book of World Records*. (I think a Rolls Royce Phantom cost less!)

The body was hand-formed by Ron Clark and constructed by Bob Kaiser from Clark Kaiser Customs. It has a rear-wheel drive. The chassis is a hand-formed, 125-inch wheelbase, alloy tube frame.

The design included the first backseat-mounted radio speakers, and hidden windshield wipers that started themselves when it rained. Other features included retractable headlamps, rear indicators that swiveled as the car turned, "floating" bumpers, and a trunk that was hinged from the driver's side.

Each of the four bucket seats had their own thermostatically controlled air conditioning, and there are individual cigarette lighters and ashtrays, as well as a radio speaker at each seat.

The original engine, a Cadillac V-8, was later replaced by a 427 high-performance by Ford when it was taken on the show circuit. Ironically if it were a side-oiler, as used in the 427 Cobra, the engine itself would be a collector's item today.

Darin proudly drove his wife, Sandra Dee, in the car to the 34th Academy Awards in 1961. Unfortunately, he hadn't been briefed on the cooling fans, and the car overheated. The car had two fans and a switch that you had to turn on. Bobby didn't realize that, so it heated up and smoke poured out. All the magazines said the car caught fire, but it didn't.

The car was donated to a Museum in St. Louis.

I haven't seen it at Pebble Beach, so I'm assuming it's been forgotten. Newspaper accounts say the car is worth $1 million. I say, since Bobby Darin died so young—in his '30s—and didn't have a full career like Sinatra and Tony Martin, he's largely forgotten. And so is the car. That's why there aren't more custom cars in this book, because they have no known value other than who they were identified with—if, in fact, it was a famous owner.

Looking back at what he could have bought at the time with that kind of bread—like five or six V-12 Ferraris—I gotta say, Bobby, me boy, you put your money on the wrong car...

Chapter 32
The Dirtbag Cobra Big Block (1965 427 Cobra)
Yes, it was found raggedy...

You gotta admit, with a half century or more gone by, the original CSX2000 and CSS3000 Cobras have been through hell and high water.

First there were the guys flaring out the fenders to put on wider wheels and tires, and then the rush to make the big-blocks look like an S/C, a sort of street/competition model made from leftover unsold race cars, and then candy colors, and then polishing to bare metal—not to mention smashups, and rollovers, and burned-to-the-ground stories.

So it's rare to find one that is *as found* unmolested, except by the ravages of time, so to speak.

First a little bit of history about the big-block Cobra.

Shelby, of course, started out with the small-block 260, then upgraded to the 289, though still a Cobra with leaf springs. But

the 289 Cobra still couldn't catch the Ferraris, so he authorized his mechanics to stuff a 390 into a leaf-spring car. That car was nearly uncontrollable, so Ford authorized the design of a coil-spring frame back in Dearborn.

That started the 427 Cobra, still with chassis and body built on The Olde Sode (the body hammered out "by winos under bridges," Shelby often joked)

The original engine was the FE-series side-oiler 427, a brute of an engine normally found in NASCAR stockers and some Galaxie 500 road cars. Shelby chose that engine because it could crank out 100 more horsepower than the 289 ever could on its best day. Shelby had to widen the original Cobra chassis design and make the mainframe tubes larger.

The first 100 were to be competition cars. But you had to make 100 to receive FIA homologation as a production sports car. Wouldn'tcha know it, when the inspector from the FIA showed up, only 51 cars had been completed.

So the FIA inspector refused homologation and instantly the market for 427 Cobra race cars disappeared because then buyers would have to run against prototypes that were pure race cars, faster and lighter. But, praise God, some Shelby marketing guy thought, Hell, let's put some street equipment back on—windshield and such—and call it the S/C, for "street completion."

That same ploy was used by Jaguar earlier when they had built too many D-Type Jags. They added a glass windscreen, side windows, exhaust pipes, etc., and re-named the leftovers as the XK-SS.

Similar tactics were employed at Shelby. Colin Comer, the Cobra historian, says 29 S/C cars were sold for about $8500, compared to the pure street cars that were sold for $7500. (Never you mind that some of the buyers of street cars unknowingly got weaker 428 engines, that's another story.)

This '65 Cobra 427 S/C popped up online at http://www.hemmings.com/after it was shown at various car shows in California, including one at the Petersen Museum on Wilshire Boulevard.

What's weird about the car is that it is Hertz Gold, apparently painted that way by Hertz, which was renting out Hertz Mustangs back then and wanted a tie-in. I don't know if they ever actually rented out the 427 Cobras.

It is CSX3047, which is one of only about 30 S/C's to have been produced in 1965, and one of only two in Hertz Gold, the other having already been fully restored.

"RODE HARD AND PUT AWAY WET"

From what the owner wrote on a sign he shows with the car, it was originally purchased by a resident of Hudson (others say Millbrook), New York, in 1966. The initial order for the car came to Shelby American from Larsen Ford of White Plains, New York, in May of 1966, and it is believed that the dealership requested the car in Hertz Gold, for promotional advertising purposes, and that the dealership was invoiced $7,395 upon delivery. So they probably sold it for above that if they were in the profit-making business. On the other hand, they might have sold it for cost once they got their promotional time out of its carcass.

After being sold to a private customer, it was brought it back to the dealership a month later to have warranty work performed. Among the items: replacement of a broken pushrod and a damaged lifter, and rebuilding the heads. Out in the west, when I was wrangling horses, we'd have said it had been "rode hard and put away wet."

The car went through more owners. The third one lived north of the border in Ontario, Canada, and offered the Cobra for sale in December, 1970. He was unschooled in Cobra history (hey, I didn't write *Shelby's Wildlife* until 1977), so he described it as one of just 25 "street/competition" models, but added that it had a blueprinted LeMans engine (under warranty) and "no history of competition use or damage."

It then passed to a memorable owner named Carter Gette.

Carter Gette thought of a way to make money with the car. Maybe Hertz wouldn't rent it, but he sure as well would, so he offered it up at Lime Rock for $200 per weekend. Such a deal, right? Uh, but he was also demanding a $10,000 deposit to cover any possible damage. Gette (not related to the California Getty family) was a character after my own heart. A pedal-to-the-metal, let-the-devil-take-the-hindmost kinda guy. According to letter I received in April, 2015, from a friend of his, Chauncy Johnstone:

Gette also owned Donzi Boats. He drove very fast and hard. I believe he raced the Cobra a few times at the Dover Drag strip, but never in a road race. The Gette Ford franchise was obtained with the assistance of some high-level Ford executive that Robert Gette, Carter's Dad, had recruited. Carter's Dad passed away last year.

Around 1969, Carter, myself, some friends, and Paul Newman, a neighbor, met at one of the practice days at Lime Rock. I drove the car there, as did Carter, and also Newman. Newman did not care much for the Cobra when he drove it, finding it based on power but not finesse. I drove it in a Gymkhana in Kahtona, NY. It was a beast to handle.

Carter was severely injured in a motorcycle accident in June of 1970. He had a 4-cylinder Honda and hit, of all things, a Mustang that was backing out of a driveway. He hit the car broadside and totaled it, which gives you an idea of how fast he was going. Upon hearing the news, I immediately rushed, with another friend, to the Vassar Hospital. Carter was a mess. I nearly passed out when I saw him. I recall him telling me, "Don't worry Chaunce, I'll be out of here in a week." Carter suffered from the results of that accident, and was taking painkillers for the rest of his life. He passed away in 2003.

Carter still owned the Cobra in 1972. I know this because he came to my new home in Wilton, CT, and took me for a ride. I was concerned because of his accident problems and the telephone poles looked like a picket fence.

Carter got into Porsches and his last car was a Porsche 911 GT 2. Carter had lost his license by then and I had to drive the car with him in it. He was a great friend.

Gette found a monied individual named Richard Reventlow (yes, from that family, the brother of Bruce, developer of the Scarab and Shelby's one time landlord) but Reventlow only kept it a few months, then returned it and got all his money back!

Johnstone 's last memory of the car was it being sold by Gette to someone in Westport, Connecticut. When later owner Don Silawky decided in 2005 that it was time to remove the blue paint, he did so, only to find the gold paint underneath. He was gratified to find out it had no huge amounts of Bondo, as some Cobras do.

Even the Cobra's period-correct magnesium knock-off wheels were on the car, which was amazing, since they are the most fragile part of the car. The car was also found with its original soft top, tonneau cover, side curtains, and seat belts.

After a 40-year period in the "barn," so to speak (hey, all you barn-find writers, most barn-finds today are found in garages), it was purchased by a California-based enthusiast who immediately began showing it unrestored, warts and all, which was very educational because usually, when a Cobra has been re-painted (perhaps the wrong color) and reupholstered (perhaps the wrong pattern), it is no longer representative of the way they rolled out of the Shelby American factory.

And one website complemented the fact that it didn't have "a completely unnecessary signature on it's glovebox, which speaks volumes in and of itself. The sad thing is, when Carroll Shelby was alive he would even sign replica Cobra gloveboxes, so his signature does not speak of the bona fide provenance of the car." Good quote but, in fact, S/C's did not have gloveboxes!

This writer has been unable to find out what the owner paid for the car, but rest assured he paid top dollar, since on the entire planet Earth there were probably only one or two S/C

Cobras still in the barn (say, I know of one in the South Pacific but that's another story). Ironically, he already owned another genuine S/C, so he more than anyone knew the going price.

So howizit, then, that a car that sold for top dollar is in this book? For two reasons. First, even if the buyer paid $1 million, it matters not, because this represents an original *as found*. Not repainted (or at least we are to believe most of the blue paint fell off). Not reupholstered. One critic on a website pointed out numerous little things that were "wrong" like valve covers, but gimme a break, this car went through several owners. It's lucky it suffered so little replacement of small items. So what if little things were replaced—the basic frame is there unmolested and the basic body there, as per original. All the "incorrect" details pointed out by the critics can be corrected in a day.

So what that owner was paying top dollar for what, in effect, was a hunka, hunka burning love, a piece of Shelby-American history writ large. I'd say if it does go to auction, you can start at two million. And hold the carnauba wax, boys...

Chapter 33
The Cars That Never Were, Part 1: The Bentley Java (1994 Bentley Java)
Unless of course, you were a Prince...

What Bentley was trying to do, back in the early '90s, was make a smaller car. But they didn't have a smaller platform so, for a prototype, they used a BMW 5-series.

The company's styling team was led by Graham Hull in conjunction with experts from an outside company, Design Research Associates. The result was the Java, a fast, comfortable car that would have opened a new market for Bentley, and probably moved the age component of its buyers demographic makeup down a good ten years.

Of course, Bentley wanted to have its own engine, not one the press would say was a modified BMW, so a V-8 engine of 3.5-liter capacity was developed by Cosworth Engineering, a subsidiary of Vickers and already successful at doing Formula 1 engines. Though the engine would have been smaller than normal Bentley engines, twin turbochargers gave it a top end in excess of 170 mph (273 km/h), though it probably would have been limited electronically to 155 mph (250 km/h).

All a great idea, but then BMW got contracts to supply a range of engines for the future Rolls-Royce Silver Seraph and Bentley Arnage models, and thus were tied up with that and the Java was left hanging.

Well almost.

That irrepressible Malaysian lover of cars, Prince Jefri, who is reported to have amassed over 3000 cars, including many one-offs, saw the prototype and ordered several. Looking at pictures of the ones he got, I can see a change in style of the Java, but maybe for the better. The Java show car looks like a Volvo convertible with a Bentley grille and Bentley taillights, where the ones built for the prince look like they have their own distinctive style.

According to the website BentleySpotting.com, the sultan owns:

BENTLEY JAVA P700 BQ7878 SCBVH99C8RCH00480
BENTLEY JAVA P710 BQ9222 SCBVH99C5TCH00492
BENTLEY JAVA BS9997 SCBVH99C4TCH00497
and ten other Bentley Javas.

The world's supply, so to speak. The website goes on to picture Bentley Java Estates (what we philistine Americans call "station wagons") and at least one coupe. Even though Bentley did not go on and produce them for commoners, the design cues developed for the Java appeared on later Bentleys like the Azure.

As it turned out, VW bought Bentley and BMW bought Rolls and a smaller Bentley, the GTC, was eventually developed, though it wasn't as small as the Java.

Prince Jefri's meddling in the normal order of things had a bright side: he didn't get those cars cheap, and it was petrodollars from Brunei that kept Bentley alive during some of the bad years. In a way, you have to consider Prince Jefri as much a "patron of the arts" as the Medici family was in hiring Leonardo da Vinci and Michelangelo to create art for them. Those patrons can certainly get things done.

Lesson learned: when you see that sign "concept car," sometimes it doesn't mean someone with a very big wallet didn't belly up to the bar and buy just one. This guy, for example, bought several. Later on, Prince Jefri's proliferate spending was curbed, and a number of the cars may have been parked, and Indonesia has high humidity so, if you want to try to bag a Java or another toy, should they come up for sale, you'll have to beat the Tin Worm.

Chapter 34
The JagZag
(1954 Jaguar XK140 Zagato Coupe)
Hey, the Italians had to show the Brits how to shape a sports car...

The Jaguar XK120—a two-seat sports car—was a big hit. It stole the London Motor Show with it's curvy voluptuous body, 160-horsepower XK engine, and 120 mph top speed—which is how, incidentally, it got its name.

But Sir William Lyons, founder of the firm, wanted to develop other cars on the same platform, so Jaguar built some racing-only models that won LeMans outright in 1953, '55, '56, and '57. At the same time, they aimed for a bit more luxury with the XK140, which had a more powerful engine and larger interior. The end of the series was the XK150, which reached 265 bhp in its ultimate form.

ITALIANO CAT

But Italians being Italians, the Jaguar dealer in Italy, Guido Modiano, wanted to see what an Italian coachbuilder could do with a Jag. He waited until an XK140 was bent and then, rather than replace the UK sheet metal, commissioned Carrozzeria Zagato to make an all-new design.

And, while you're at it, might as well give it a suede interior.

That's version 1, but there's an alternate story, maybe from an alternate universe, that, when the original Italian owner of this Jaguar XK140 got into a major accident, he took it not to a body shop but, because he was a personal friend of Ugo Zagato, he inquired about simply rebodying the car rather than repairing it. Zagato went for it because it was a chassis he would not have to buy. No doubt, Zagato was hoping he could sell Jaguar on the idea of a limited run of cars, as he had just done with Aston Martin with the DB4GTZ.

When the car was done, Modiano or Zagato (depending on which story you want to believe) took what he called the "XKZ" to the 1957 Paris Auto Salon. He intended to take orders. A brochure was made up later for a second car, a Zagato XK150 conversion shown at the 1958 Geneva Auto Show. Unfortunately, that was all she wrote. Two Jags came out of Zagato and that was the last anybody heard of them for a while.

Flash forward a few decades.

Scott Gauthier, a famous jeweler in the Southwest who was deep into Jaguars, found and bought the once-lost ZK140 (another name for it) out of a car service garage in Florida. He didn't name the price, but bought it partly disassembled, even the suede upholstery was in boxes. He took it to Italy to be restored, and it was completed in time for the 2003 Pebble Beach Concours. He took second in class, and subsequently drove the car many miles.

The JagZag, as it is affectionately called, remains a unique XK140—a reminder of how Jaguar could have become more Continental if only they had thought to imitate Aston. One amusing story is that, during its restoration in the early 2000s, traces of bent chassis from the original crash were found. But it was decided, since they were not affecting the car's structural integrity, to leave them untouched—after all they were part and parcel of the car's unique story.

Lesson to be learned? You see an old picture in *Road & Track*, some moldy old issue, and almost dismiss it, saying, surely that car was around 50 years ago, but it couldn't still be around today, could it?

Well, Scott Gauthier had probably seen that picture years earlier and parked it in a corner of his brain, so when he saw the car later he knew it was something special. No doubt, someone in Florida had taken it to a shop that didn't have the skills to repair it. Gauthier was ready and willing to take it to someone who could and, as a result, owns a very unique car.

So the lesson is: start that file of unique cars. Not all of them hit the crusher—it's your job to hunt them down, even if it's only one at a time.

Chapter 35
The Elusive Ford Mustang Wagon
(1965 Mustang)
An ad writer made a great splash with this Italian modified 'Stang, but where is it now?

Let's say you are an aggressive ad man, which, by all accounts Barney Clark was.

I was a copywriter in Detroit in another life (the "*Mad Men*" era) and remember even then he was spoken of in hushed tones for having written the Corvette ad headline "The Real McCoy," implying the previously boulevardier Corvette was now, by golly, a real sports car that could go toe-to-toe with the furrin' stuff.

Let's say you want to get some attention in your field as a aficionado, a real car enthusiast, one who has, as my friend, car designer Bill Mitchell used to say, "gasoline running in his veins."

I can understand that; I was writing Corvette ads once and was known as the "car nut" of the writing group, owning back then a Mercedes gullwing

According to an article by David E. Davis in *Car & Driver*, Barney Clark was a writer, but one who "would prefer to be an automotive designer, or an architect, or an ill-tempered mystic." He described Clark as a real radical in a three-piece suit, saying, "Barney Clark is a one-man Berkeley Student Revolution trying to set a world record for the quarter-mile in a flathead Morris Minor."

One day, Clark wanted to get a little publicity, and have a little fun, and his prescription for that was to take a humdrum car and have it redesigned in Italy. Here is Davis's account:

> *When Clark decided to re-do a production car, he chose an already popular car, the Mustang notchback. He was building what the Brits used to call a "shooting brake." I finally found out what that means. When Brits used to have only wagons (before cars) they tamed down a horse by having him tow a large heavy wagon, thus the wagon was the "brake." The shooting part was added when m'Lord would take the wagon, presumably with the horse pulling it, out on his vast estate to shoot grouse and what-not. Hence the term "shooting brake."*
>
> *In the Sixties there were a few Aston Martins converted to "shooting brakes" so m'Lord could combine hunting and sports cars, which makes perfect sense to me. (In the west, we often shoot out of our cars; at anything that moves...) Clark's collaborator in this crime was Bob Cumberford, once a GM Styling staff member who worked on special projects like the Corvette SS race car that raced at Sebring. He has an interesting background as well. He worked at GM but was shown the door when he was a little too ambitious (trying to show his designs directly to Harley Earl.)*

Davis said the inspiration for the Mustang wagon was the original Chevrolet Nomad—a two-door station wagon of the mid-Fifties, which was produced from '55 to '57.

Davis also noted that, previous to this Mustang, Clark had put together a "sleeper" '55 Chevy wagon with Corvette-type engine and suspension modifications, a subject which is a whole different kettle of fish (I'll write something about "sleepers" later).

The car they used for the Mustang wagon was a 1964 1/2 Mustang coupe, with a 260-horsepower 289 V-8 engine and automatic transmission.

Cumberford was chosen because he loved freelance projects and because he had established a working relationship with Hungarian-born engineer Frank Reisner of Intermeccanica in Turin when they designed (or re-designed, depending on who is telling the story) the car originally known as the Griffith GT *(C/D,* July '66). It later became known as the Italia.

Reisner was handed Cumberford's design for the Mustang wagon, and was very imaginative in how he worked it out. He merely removed the stock roof and rear deck, then fabricated a new roof, a new tailgate, rear windows, a cargo floor, and a folding rear seat. The Mustang wagon emerged with a fully disappearing tailgate window.

The original plan called for redesigning the gas tank and spare tire location so they could lower the cargo floor and increase the available load space, but the money well ran dry. Had there been orders for the car when people saw it at the car shows, though...

The car went to Italy in March, 1965, and arrived back in New York in February, 1966.

Clark, being a closet hot rodder, gave it a few mods, including some '66 and '67 Mustang GT exterior trim, Koni shock absorbers, Ford's optional mag-type wheels that look Shelbyesque to me, and Pirelli Cinturato radial-ply tires to improve its handling and braking performance.

Davis was privileged to drive it over a thousand miles, and recalled "people actually waved us to the side of the road to ask us about it."

True, the car would never score well in cargo room, the payload space measuring roughly 44 inches wide and 36 inches deep with the rear seat down.

Davis wrote that Clark and Cumberford's ambition at the time was to build Mustang wagons as a commercial venture but, even though Davis said the public response was "spectacular," this writer knows of no follow-ups built in Italy—though I have seen customs imitating the design at the Fabulous Fords Forever show in Buena Park, California. (GM had clay models of Camaro wagons, so they were ready to fight back had Ford put this design into production.)

Davis got a kick out of describing a GM employee's reaction to the car:

> *In fact, some poor GM type who knew of his company's top-secret experiments in this area got the shock of his life one morning when he saw Barney's fully-appointed, apparently-production, '66 Mustang wagon whizzing along Detroit's Southfield Expressway. Within an hour telephones were ringing all over the Motor City as various firms' intelligence agents tried to ferret out the truth about this latest bombshell from Dearborn.*
>
> *As far as Barney was concerned, that alone was worth the time, trouble, and expense. His enemies were confounded.*
>
> *So, in effect, it was all some grand cosmic joke played on his former taskmasters at GM through the agency. I think he should have gone full-tilt boogie and fabricated fake manufacturer's plates to really set tongues a-waggin'.*

In a 2011 article posted on *Mustangs&Fords.com*, Brad Bowling writes that Ford, in fact, already had clay models of 1965 Mustang wagons but were so busy selling coupes and convertibles they didn't want to take up time doing a wagon.

Now those whose primary attitude is impatience will dismiss any thought that this car could still exist. But on the net, in a matter of minutes, I found a picture of the car parked in front of someone's house, indicating it had daily use. I believe it had New Jersey plates, the numbers something like 4600. But I can't read the first two letters. (Hey *you* have to do a *little* bit of work, too...) There are no doubt services that can track down old license plates and give you an address the plate was registered to.

That's a place to start. Or run pictures of it in Mustang club magazines on the east coast promising a reward for information on its location.

Hey, it was too darn unique to throw away, and if it were a custom done in America this chapter wouldn't be here. But Italy—ah-h-h, *now* you're talkin'. Pass the *vino*...

Chapter 36
The Gullwinged Pontiac
(1954 Bonneville Special)
It coulda hurt the Corvette...

If you weren't aware there was a car called the 1954 Pontiac Bonneville Special, you might think, at first glance, it nought but a customized Corvette. But no, this car was built under the order of GM VP in charge of Styling Harley Earl, who had two-seat show cars built to showcase in each division: Cadillac, Olds, Buick and Chevrolet. Only the Chevrolet-badged version, the Corvette, made it into production.

Where a lot of GM dream cars dredged up visions of European racing names, this one harkened images of folks vying for speed records on Utah's Bonneville Salt Flats. The designers credited with its shape were Homer LaGassey and Paul Gilland and you can see by the amount of chrome it was meant to sell at a higher price than the Corvette if it was ever produced.

Only two were built. One sold at auction in 2006 for $3.08 million, and later returned to the block in Scottsdale, Arizona, as part of Barrett-Jackson's Ron Pratte Collection sale.

The Bonneville Special went beyond the Corvette by having a bubble cockpit with flip up side windows. The Corvette had bubble tops experimentally, but not in production.

The first two years of the Corvette saw an inline six, but the '55 had an optional V-8. It seems odd, then, if they were thinking of going up against the Corvette, that GM bosses chose to have a straight eight under the Bonneville Special's hood. The 268-cubic-inch, inline-eight-cylinder engine looked exotic though—fitted as it was with four side-draft carburetors—and GM claimed it was good for 230 horsepower.

The car had a lot of design cues found in other Earl designs, such as floors with brushed aluminum surfaces and rubber ridges for traction, and a shifter for the Hydra-Matic automatic transmission that resembled a lever you would find in a plane to raise and lower landing gear. Earl was ga-ga over airplane instruments, so the Bonneville Special included a whole raft of gauges, including a clock, compass, and manifold temperature gauge—all, rumors say, sourced from an aircraft salvage dealer.

Apparently the first car, a non-functioning pushmobile, was red, with the follow up car metallic green. Both had numerous aircraft-inspired touches, like faux oil coolers, machined from aluminum billet, mounted on each fender. A throwback to pre-war styling was the functional Continental wheel kit—shaped a bit like the exhaust outlet of a fighter jet. (You have to remember: this is when air forces were still switching from prop planes to jet fighters and anything that reminded people of jets was exciting.)

The first Bonneville Special made its debut in January, 1954, at the New York City Motorama, an event always held at the Waldorf-Astoria Hotel. The crowd liked it so much, funds were budgeted for a second car, which made its debut at the March, 1954, Motorama, held at the Pan-Pacific Auditorium in Los Angeles. That car was the one painted metallic green. It had a few less gauges, Earl having calmed down a bit. This second one was a fully functional car. After appearing at all the Motoramas, it was sent on a tour of various dealers to bring in showroom traffic.

Motorama historian David W. Temple said in his book, *GM's Motorama*, that the Bonneville Specials were scheduled to be destroyed when their tours were over, but were saved. How Joe Bortz, the Chicago collector, got one is simple—he bought it from the Detroit Historical Society, which runs a Museum on Woodward Ave. It has at least half a dozen former show cars, but not enough money or space to display them. (The author would like to know what it sold for at auction, and in what year, so if anyone knows...)

How owning No. 1 led to No. 2 is an interesting story. What happened was that he was showing No. 1 when some bloke pops up and says, "I know where No. 2 is." So Bortz bought that as well. He later sold to Denver collector Roger Willbanks, who in turn bankrolled a ground-up resto just in time for the 2000 Meadow Brook Concours d'Elegance. In 2006, that same car was bought by Ron Pratte at Barrett-Jackson's Scottsdale, Arizona, sale and more recently was auctioned again.

The purpose of the Bonneville Specials was to liven up Pontiac's image, and that they did. While the design never saw production, the two cars buffed up the carmaker's image, keeping Pontiac in business until they got serious enough to make production-model high-performance cars like the 1964 GTO.

One could even stretch the contribution of the Bonneville Special to saying it inspired the Pontiac Solstice, a two-seat convertible (and later, coupe) produced from 2005-2010 that had the samelong hood and pontoon-style front fenders. Though the Solstice designer hadn't even been born when the Bonneville Special was being shown, it seems he channeled the experience and produced a similar car.

Lesson learned? Joe Bortz proved there is more than one way to find a car. Put out bait. Buy what you want in any condition and maybe if there's more people that have one they will come to you. Hey, I know it works from a guy who had a Delahaye. He was showing it at Pebble Beach and a guy walked up and said, "I know where there's another one of those." My pal bought it.

Chapter 37
The Strange But True Story of a LeMans racing Porsche that Got Lost (and found) (1951 356 SL Gmünd Coupé)
Once I was lost; now I am found...

It is a bit ironic that after designing such thunderous heavy-weight racers as the Mercedes SSK before the war, Professor Porsche designed some small cars and began marketing them under his own name when he began his postwar career.

The first was an open car but then he did an aerodynamic coupe (these are the postwar cars, though he did do a VW-based prewar aerodynamic study). Though that first postwar spyder had the engine amidships it was decided to put the engine behind the rear wheels in the production models.

GMUND SAWMILL
It was in an abandoned Gmund, Austria sawmill that they started building the first Porsche cars for sale.

The first coupe rolled out the door in June 1948 and by mid-1949 more than forty had been finished and shipped out to dealers. Those Austrian-built ones had lightweight bodywork of aluminum, hand beaten panels to match a wood "former" and then welded together. That somewhat limited production, they only had three guys that could hand beat aluminum, and the best one had to be searched for on occasion in the local bars and sobered up.

Later on when they got rolling, they moved to a Stuttgart suburb, Zuffenhausen, assigning a coachbuilder there, Reutter, to build the coachwork but this time of steel.

Originally the goal was to sell street cars but with the racing background, everybody expected Porsche to build some race cars. So since they had some aluminum coachwork already built in the Gmund cars (they had saved eleven bodies) , they built race cars of them dubbed the *Super Liecht* (SL) or Sport Light cars, which were easily 200 lbs. less than a Stuttgart built 356 steel car.

Porsche was not shy, their attitude being if they were going to race they were prepared to go after the Big Dogs and accordingly they built three SL Coupes for their first outing at LeMans, in 195. Two of the three crashed in practice. But the one with the number 46 on the door, driven by French drivers Auguste Veuillet and Edmond Mouche took first in the 1100 class in the other one, marking the first victory for a German sports car in international racing after the war.

After Le Mans, Liege Rome Liege, and Montlhery the SL was entered in a French race called Coupe du Salon in October of 1951 driven by none other than the cars successful Le Mans pilot August Veuillet.

NEW GLORY IN AMERICA

In an ideal world, a car that accomplished so much for them–SN 063--the LeMans car--would be honored, put in the Porsche Museum. But in those days, Porsche's priority was getting new cars out the door and the LeMans coupe was sold to their American distributor Max Hoffman. Hoffman sold 356/2-063 to Johnny Von Neumann in 1952, Von Neumann being his West Coast distributor, running a dealership called Competition Motors in North Hollywood, California. He not only sold Porsches, he raced them.

Following a practice session at Palm Springs in March 23, 1952, he entered the coupe in the April 20th Pebble Beach races with silver body and dark blue hood color, then ran the Golden Gate Park race on May 31st with the coupe re-painted red. Following this he had Emil Diedt in Southern California turn the car into a red roadster prior to the July 20, Torrey Pines, Ca race. He then went all the way to Wisconsin to compete in the September 6 Elkhart Lake, WI.

He next raced it September 10 in Costa Mesa, Ca, and then racked up two more races in Calif. One at Modesto, and the last at Torrey Pines, Ca. He sold the car in December 1952 .

It was at Torrey Pines (a course near San Diego) in where Von Neumann won the first race in the US for the Porsche marque. Back then you didn't think about preserving originality and he installed production brakes which were larger and ran the car without the front fender skirts which were really only needed on a long track like LeMans.

But the big Crime Against Originality (what is the sentence for that in the Porsche world? Death?) was that he hacked the roof off.As a roadster the car was very light-- 1385 lbs.

Von Neumann sold the car in 1952 to Bill Wittington of Woodside, California.

Wittington ran the car at Salt Lake City, Utah and again at the Golden Gate races (through Golden Gate park in San Francisco) in 1953.

The next year it had another owner--Rick Gale –who had Ed Phelan race it at Golden Gate Park in 1954. Another well-known owner of the time was starting in '54, Ernie Spritzer who raced the car at Santa Rosa, California. Spitzer took it to the body shop of Gorden Vann in Berkeley for maintenance and while there the cowl was reshaped, a new dashboard installed and yet another color was prescribed for it, this time yellow.

AN OWNER MAKING HISTORY

Now by the mid-'50s, ya think someone would have noticed the car's provenance, aluminum body and all that. But no, the next guy that bought it, in 1957, was Chuck Forge who graduated from Stanford with an EE degree and went to work for Hewlett-Packard. Once he was getting paychecks he had the credit to buy the ex-Von Neumann roadster. By then the Porsche motor was dead so he did what you did back then—threw in new VW engine so he could drive it on the street as well as autocross it once in a while.

He still had the original engine and rebuilt the 1500cc Super. This car was competing in his garage with a racing Corvair, a 1957 Porsche Carrera Coupe and a hot-rodded beetle.

One thing he added to the car was the rear skirts, as it ran at LeMans, and eventually uniting those with the front skirts again. He said he was never going to part with it, and a man true to his word, he didn't, the car being sold after his death in 2010.

NEW OWNER, THE ROOF RETURNS

The new owner was Cameron Healy, who took the car to be restored to master 356 builder Rod Emory. As they took the car apart and found it was chassis number 63, they were rocked back on their heels because this was a historic car—the first Porsche to ever take honors at Le Mans.

Now some barn finders would at that point be motivated to sell their find, now that its true pedigree was known. But Cameron hung in there, determined to restore the car to its original state.

Choosing Rod Emory was fortuitous because the Emory family was involved with Porsches since the Fifties. They use both classic antique methods of restoration and modern computer aided design.

The decision was made to return the car to its original state as far as cosmetics, meaning you see actual imperfections of hand production, which meant hand making the original panels that had been removed when it was cut down into a roadster. Two SL cars and two Gmund street cars we accessed for roof research. As each car was built by hand there are subtle differences in each roof line and as a result the Le Mans SL was completed with it's own specific roof design. Several Porsche SLs were measured so the new bodywork would be a match, though of course in the hand done days at Gmund, each car was individual as well.

A 1.1 liter engine was built for it so it is as much as possible like the car that sat on the grid at LeMans in 1951.

In 2015 the restored car was shown at Rennsport V in Monterey. It was later loaned to the Porsche Museum.

Lesson to be learned? Often you will find that racers back at that time, before vintage racing, God luv 'em, sometimes didn't give a fig for originality. Naw, they just want something fast. So in planning your barn finding, be sure to beat the bushes for old race drivers so you can see what they still got stored in the barn. Chuck Forge had this treasure for decades but no one seemed to notice it was a LeMans racer in its first incarnation.....now that it's been unearthed that only 7 or 8 Gmunds can be tied to factory racing, the find is that much more significant.

Chapter 38
From Coupe to Spyder to Coupe, Starring Steve McQueen
(1967 Ferrari 275 GTB coupe)
The "McQueen Effect" takes hold once more...

Now when you are Steve McQueen, highest grossing film star for a certain number of years, you got clout.

We call it "star power."

And, even though Steve McQueen has been dead for many years, just the fact that he owned a certain car is now—time after time—translating to bigger dollars at the major auctions.

This is the story of the King of Cool's interlude with the NART Spyder.

First of all, who be NART? They be the North American Racing Team, started by Luigi Chinetti, Sr., who won LeMans for Ferrari in 1949, more or less putting the firm in the spotlight. And they be his son, Luigi, Jr. ("Coco"), who has always been on the more creative side of the operation, thinking up new designs.

It was Luigi, Jr., who, on seeing Ferrari's version of the 275 GTS, thought, No, our customers want the coupe-body styling, and ordered ten coupes cut into spyders. Ferrari resisted at first but, once the Chinettis ordered ten coupes and paid for them, he could do nothing. So the Chinettis sent the coupes to Scaglietti, then still semi-independent of Ferrari, to have them cut down into NART Spyders.

The very first one, 09437, you might have seen if you ever watched the film *The Thomas Crown Affair*, with McQueen playing a wealthy financier/con man (aren't they all?) opposite Faye Dunaway.

MCQUEEN ORDERS HIS OWN

That's when McQueen must have gotten the bug for owning a NART Spyder, because he ordered one—SN 10453—and had it sent to Junior Conway, a famous car painter and body man, and had the rear spoiler and competition-style Monza quick-fill snap-open gas cap added. He got to enjoy it for but a day or two before he got into a wreck on the Pacific Coast Highway driving back to his Malibu home.

The rumor is that a truck driver, seeing two pretty girls walking across the road to the beach, was distracted enough to plow into the dark blue McQueen Spyder. (I'll admit to being distracted on the same highway by the same sight, only I'll admit it just took one babe in a bikini to draw my eye from the business of driving.)

The car was taken to Hollywood Sports Cars and their body man began. Bear in mind there were no spare parts for the NART Spyder body; everything had been hand-made in Italy.

Steve McQueen was an impatient man. He couldn't wait for replacement parts to be made, whether here or in the old country. He thereupon bought a red 275 GTB/4 from Modern Classic Motors in Reno, this time a coupe, red with black interior, and had it cut down. This may have been serial number 10621.

He drove this hybrid for awhile and finally sold it in 1971. Who should buy it but another movie star, in this case *Zorro* and *Lost in Space* star Guy Williams, who traded in a Maserati 3500 GT for it. He owned it for five years.

In 1976, the four-cam car changed hands again, this time, according to RM Auction Co., going to J.P. Hyan, who encountered rear-end damage, so it went back to Conway's House of Color and sat for some years until California-based trucking magnate Robert Panella bought it in October, 1980, for $32,000.

At that time, the car had roughly 20,000 miles on the odometer, so, mechanically, it was far from being used up.

CONVERSION TO SPYDER

We will never know why people want to cut coupes into spyders. I think the fact there were only ten NART Spyders makes them more desirable, even if they were cars cut later. Panella put it under the knife, which at that time cost only $10,000, and had the best man in the U.S. do it: Richard Straman, in Costa Mesa, California. (RM says he used Scaglietti's own bucks—I doubt that...).

Panella had it painted fly yellow, and it was once again recalling the car in *The Thomas Crown Affair*. It then went to Erick Zausner, who kept it for four years until it went to England, to Andrew Pisker.

The car's next journey was to Australia, where 1983 Le Mans winner Vern Schuppan alerted yachtsman and historic racer Peter Harburg to the car's availability. In fact, Schuppan liked it so much he bought it in 2009.

As a McQueen fan, he wanted to bring the car back to original. To his credit (if you're a staunch originality fan), he didn't mean "original" as keeping it in a spyder configuration, because McQueen never owned that particular chassis when it was a spyder.

BACK TO COUPE

By "original," he meant making it a coupe again.

Well, there you had a problem. Because, where once there were half a dozen conversion shops cutting roofs off of Ferraris, nobody ever saved the tops, with their precious rear window glass.

Fortunately, Ferrari had set up a restoration workshop called *Ferrari Classiche* in Maranello, Italy. RM Auctions says that parts removed during the N.A.R.T. conversion "were located by Schuppan and reinstalled by Ferrari, including the pristine rear glass and chrome surround, the rear deck (trunk lid), and the internal roof buttress metal pressings. In order to achieve perfect alignment and fit of the roof panel, Ferrari's experts built a full custom body jig."

Of course, Ferrari had the factory records, and were able to find the original color (Nocciola) but it was decided to return it to what the owner called "McQueen spec" (Chianti Red), based on a color swatch provided by Lee Brown himself, the very same body shop owner who had painted it that color for McQueen.

The decision to go back to a coupe paid off. The car sold at the RM auction at Monterey in 2014 for $10,175,000—a high price for a 275 GTB/4 at the time but, hey, this one was both owned and driven by the King of Cool.

On the Ferrari fan site Ferrarichat.com, there was much discussion about whether the result can be considered "original," but to me this was all a tempest in a teapot, since the 275 GTBs were built during the hand-built era at Ferrari and, if it is Ferrari themselves later restoring the car at Ferrari, then it is still the same automaker building the same car.

Lesson to be learned? There were probably those who passed up on the opportunity to buy this car earlier, knowing it had been "cut" into a spyder by an American conversion shop long after the run of Chinetti-ordered 275 NART Spyders had been built. So it was, in that sense, a "replica" of something that had originally been done in Italy. Some might have wanted it if it had been a coupe but, once the top was cut, there were no shops here or there converting spyders back into coupes.

Then two things happened to change the equation. First, 275 GTB coupes climbed steadily in price so, eventually, the idea of converting spyders didn't seem like a waste of money.

The second thing that happened was the "McQueen Effect," first noticed when a Ferrari Lusso owned by Steve McQueen went up for auction and sold for far more than the auction house expected it to sell for because, by that time, the image of McQueen—even though he had been dead for decades—was being used to sell books, watches, DVDs of his old films, etc. McQueen was cool again—and so was everything ever owned by him.

Lesson learned? First look at a given car apart from any mention of previous owners. See how original it is. Then, and only then, should you consider provenance (and I'm talking *any* rare car, not just a Ferrari). Some previous owners' names will ring bells with the public, others not so much. It's largely a matter of age. I remember stars people half my age never heard of. They couldn't give a damn, so I shouldn't let my admiration for some past star like James Coburn or Jack Palance impel me to buy a car that is otherwise priced too high.

I still say the DNA of the car—its bones, so to speak—are fundamentally what counts. This was still a 275 GTB chassis with the right engine and right gearbox, so no matter how much the exterior was diddled with by previous owners, I say it was "well bought" by the owner who took it to restoration. There are strict constructionists (to use a phrase normally used for describing a way the Supreme Court should interpret the U.S. Constitution) who say any bodywork done after the car was originally made makes it unoriginal, but you won't find me in that camp. A car's body is only the clothing it wears at specific times. This car went from coupe to spyder to coupe, and the decision to go back to original—with the work done by those whose name is on the car's nameplate—was its saving grace.

Chapter 39
The Hudson Initiative
(1955 Hudson Italia)
Before Exner, another Detroit Automaker was building cars in Italy

It is thought by many that Virgil Exner, Sr., was the man who, in the 1950s, opened the door for Italian carrozzerias to do prototypes for Detroit cars. That was because more than 18 different Chrysler and Dodge prototypes were done at Ghia.

Actually, it was another Detroit automaker, one now almost forgotten, who did a deal to body cars in Italy and bring them to the U.S., and that automaker was Hudson. Only Hudson did better than Chrysler, actually selling the Italian-bodied cars, rather than just showing dream cars you couldn't buy.

World War II had devastated many of the coachbuilders in Europe, wiped out their market so to speak, so after the war it was no longer fashionable to order a chassis first and then select a coachbuilder, as it had been among the rich before the war.

The French coachbuilders mostly disappeared, but the Italians hung on with Frua, Ghia, Vignale, Bertone, Pinin Farina, and several others doing a few prototypes a year—always hoping for that big contract from an automaker.

Detroit sold mass-produced cars, and the idea of actually making the body in Italy didn't pencil out as profitable, but American automakers did consult the Italians when it came to special-bodied show cars.

At the time, Hudson was a player in the American high-performance car niche with its '48 uni-body car, nicknamed the "Step Down," thanks to its low-slung design. The car had good handling and dominated NASCAR three years in a row, starting from 1951.

ITALY THE ANSWER?

A second variation, somewhat smaller, the Jet, was introduced in 1953. Chief designer Frank Spring knew about the Italian coachbuilders and contracted with Carrozzeria Touring of Milan to collaborate on a design for a grand touring coupe using Jet mechanicals. Comparing a Jet from Detroit to a Jet from Italy, you can see what the Italians wrought.

Touring was an old-line Italian coachbuilder, founded in 1926 by Felice Bianchi Anderloni. They were most famous before the war for the Alfa Romeo and Isotta-Fraschini cars they bodied. In the 1930s, Anderloni was the pioneer in what he called the "Superleggera" body, a super-light method of body construction, in which an aluminum body skin clothed a framework of small diameter tubes mounted on a chassis. The best examples before the war were the Alfa Romeo 8C 2900 and the BMW 328.

After the war, the most famous Touring design was the Ferrari Barchetta 166. But they also did Alfas, Lancias, Pegasos, and Aston Martins.

THE ITALIA

The Hudson Italia that Touring created in 1953 had the same jet-age inspiration as Savonuzzi's Ghia Supersonic design that was offered on the Fiat 8V, Jaguar XK120, and Aston Martin chassis. Some also cite Pinin Farina's Lancia Aurelia PF200 as an inspiration.

The Italia body was mounted to the Jet chassis and sat ten inches lower than standard Hudson models. The engine was a 114-horsepower, 201.5 cubic-inch inline six with two dual-barrel carburetors. That was connected to a three-speed manual transmission. The suspension was the usual Detroit independent-coil spring front and leaf springs to the rear. Brakes were four-wheel drums. The body was hand formed aluminum. One odd feature was the v-shaped scoops above the headlights that were functional brake cooling vents. A space-age inspiration was that the stop, tail, and back-up lights were housed in three chromed tubes on the side of each rear fender, as simulated "jet exhaust outlets."

Similar to the later GT40, the top of each door was cut into the roof 14 inches to allow easier entry to the low-slung car. Inside, there was a new kind of seating to Americans— "anatomically-designed" reclining leather buckets. And guess what, no chrome on the dashboard, the opposite of what Harley Earl was doing at GM.

Similar to Henry Ford's policy with the Model T (available in any color, as long as it's black), Italias came in only one color, though fortunately not black. No, it was an Italian cream with a red and cream interior. The Italia saw the introduction of knock-off chrome Borrani wire wheels on an Ameircan car.

The car had pretty good handling, due to a low center of gravity. I have been unable to find out how many they wanted to build, but only 26 got out the door before the great ship Hudson went down—or, more correctly, was merged with Nash.

The last thing the new management at Nash wanted when they absorbed Hudson was this odd-looking Italian-bodied car. Not only that, the car was priced at $4,350 (other reports say dealers had to pay $4,800) and lost money with every car built.

I would say the "groundswell" for Italias hasn't grown yet but, at the French and Italian Car Day in Van Nuys, I met a

Swedish resident of the U.S. who bought the 7th one made, once the Paris show car in 1954, from Sweden in October of 1999. I believe he paid $30,000 for the car in rough shape, but I am sure that it will be worth several hundred thousand when you consider that RM Auctions sold a restored one in 2009 for that amount.

A Hudson website says only 21 of the 26 made have been located. They are excellent examples of what Detroit automakers could have done if they had only developed a clientele that appreciated Italian coachwork. Instead, guys like Harley Earl ruled, with their yards of chrome and button-tufted upholstery.

Lesson to be learned? Note that I said a Swede who bought an American car in Sweden. I think most American car collectors who have been beating the bushes for years to find their dream car never even consider that the car they want might be in some foreign country. This guy had an advantage, as he had owned Hudsons before, and could speak the lingo, but I've been there, and found most Swedes can speak English. Not that Hudson Jet mechanical parts are easy to find in the U.S., but I am sure most Swedes steered clear of it, figuring they could spend the rest of their lives looking for mechanical parts.

So consider enlarging your search area beyond U.S. shores; I think Canada is the next target of opportunity. Last lesson? Don't let geography hinder your search.

Chapter 40
A Strange Spyder
(1969 Ferrari 365GTC)
Hauntingly familiar, but you can't quite place it...

It's like when those movie stars who, after being off-screen for a decade, come back to an appearance on the red carpet and nobody recognizes them.

That's the way I describe this 1969 Ferrari 365GTC Spyder, serial number 12181. First of all, it's true that Pininfarina, the design house and coachbuilder, did make 365GTSs, but their version looked completely different. In all, Ferrari made roughly 168 examples of the 365GTC, most being grand touring coupes. All had 320-horsepower, single-cam-per-bank, 4.4-liter V-12s with three Weber 40 DFI/5 carburetors

The open 365GTS build numbered just 20 cars.

But this car looks different from those. There's a good reason for that. This car was born as a coupe, then had an accident. The wreck went to the Chinettis in Connecticut. They, Ferrari dealers and a father and son team, decided to rebody it as a custom body and as an open car.

The appeal of the car is the narrow nose, the lack of front bumpers, and the unusual side vents (which alas resemble those on the much less valuable Intermeccanica Italia).

There's also the car's connection with NART, an acronym standing for North American Racing Team. NART not only distributed Ferraris in America for Enzo Ferrari but sponsored many a race team, including the one that won LeMans in 1965.

Now, when you say "NART Spyder" to Ferrari buffs, they usually picture the ten well-publicized, factory-built 275 GTB/4-based NART Spyders, one of which raced at LeMans. Another was in a Steve McQueen movie, The Thomas Crown Affair.

But those were of 1967 vintage.

Or, if you mention "365 Spyder" to someone who really knows his or her Ferraris, he or she might envision the three 365GTB/4s (also called Daytonas) made into Michelotti-bodied Spyders by NART.

But references to this car, owned by an Orange County man since 1987, are few and far between.

The owner has written proof from the builders that they were trying to do a car that had a lot of Pininfarina design cues.

Marcel Massini, the Swiss Ferrari expert, commented on the forum in FerrariChat.com back in April, 2006, about the three cars with this body style:

> "The chassis frames are from 1969, of course, as can be seen from their numbers. Three - not two - were built. The first one is S/N 12515, the other two 12605 and 12611 (as you listed them already). They were built by Carrozzeria Autosport of Bachelli & Villa in Bastiglia near Modena to a design of Luigi Chinetti Junior.
>
> I'd call them rebodies. Frames and engines are original Ferrari."

So, cheekily, Lou Chinetti, Jr., was poking Pininfarina in the ribs. Although Pininfarina was the design house which had, in the past, designed most Ferraris, he was demonstrating that more exciting cars could be built on the same chassis.

In the restyling, Chinetti added a central, twin-nostril scoop, feeding six Weber carburetors which were added after the Californian took delivery of the car. Though the engine has the same 4.4-liter displacement as the fabled four-cam Daytona, it is a single cam per bank.

In the rear, the car got a "racing look" from a centrally located competition-style aluminum snap-open gas cap. Adding it required the whole deck lid be shortened.

Young Lou Chinetti had previously commissioned dozens of one-off Ferrari restylings, on one of which he recently took his custom body off of and replaced with a stock one–then sold for a reported $10 million plus.

Some who know Ferrari engineering say the car would be more structurally prepared to be an open car if they would have used an open 365GTC, but the base coupe was far cheaper to get hold of. Besides, it had been through a fire. Which meant it was really cheap.

In 1987, someone from Orange County bought the car sight unseen and flew to New York to collect it from Lou Chinetti, Jr., in person. The car was subsequently painted by Bill DeCarr in Bellflower, California, where "Bill's Body Shop" did many an exotic car.

In 1990, DeCarr somehow got it rolled out onto the lawn at the Pebble Beach Concours d'Elegance, where it was shown in an elite class dedicated to "Special Italian Coachwork from 1958-1969." Normally, a custom body done on a car far out of time sequence and not by the automaker wouldn't make it onto the vaunted Pebble grounds, but that particular class had some other modified cars, too, such as a Ghia-bodied DeTomaso Vallelunga Competition Coupe, and one of the Scaglietti-bodied Corvette Italias (a Carroll Shelby project with Corvettes done in Italy).

Following that show, the car was sent to storage for almost two decades, only to be brought out again for concours and Ferrari events.

So it remains a mystery car, a long-running project, begun in the early 1970s, shelved following the sale of Chinetti Motors, and resumed in the early '80s. Lou Chinetti, Jr., when interviewed by Mike Daly for the October 17, 2013, issue of Forza magazine, said, "It began as a contemporary car and ended up as an antique."

It might be a car built out of time, so to speak, but it *is* a real 365GTC underneath. It is documented as a Chinetti-designed car. It is documented as being built by NART in Italy. But the timeline is different, in that it was built after the other NART cars were built, so does that make it a custom? Or will this car ever be rebodied as a 365GTC again, now that the coupes are going for almost a million dollars?

Well, one thing's for sure: it is the topic of conversation wherever it appears.

Lesson to be learned? Some cars have such deep DNA, such provenance, that they can overcome whatever bodywork changes have been wrought upon it. Like the four-cam 275GTB that McQueen owned that went from coupe to spyder to coupe. This car, if 365GTCs go past a million, could be a good buy if you consider the cost at the time as a cut car and convert it back to a coupe. No doubt some who consider themselves astute buyers could have bought it as a cut car for far less in the '80s, but who knew 365GTCs would appreciate so much?

When considering a cut car, one has to first look at the production numbers of the originals. Is it a low enough number that a cut one is worth it? Depending on what that number is, the answer could be yes. And, after all, you could always enjoy it as an open car and convert it someday down the road.

Chapter 41
Along Came a Spyder
(1971 Ferrari Daytona 365GTB/S Daytona Spyder)
Wherein a Ferrari designer is influenced by a Corvette.

Looking back at it from the perspective of 2016, you kind of wonder why a design as beautiful as the Pininfarina-designed Ferrari Daytona coupe was thrown out for one that looked like a Mako Shark-style Corvette.

Well, there's actually an answer, and one that made sense at the time. It involves the son of Luigi Chinetti, the first Ferrari importer to the U.S. Luigi, Jr., fancied himself a car designer and, for more than a decade, created special-bodied Ferraris for Americans.

In 1974, my old friend from the Ferrari Owners Club, Dan Ward, got involved with a Daytona coupe, rebodied by Michelotti, a rival carrozzeria to Pininfarina.

I haven't divined whether the younger Chinetti had input on the design. I just know he was building custom Ferraris back then—and that not all his designs have stood the test of time, with at least one being rebodied back to the stock body style it was born with.

Chassis No. 15965 started out as a standard 1972 European production Daytona, albeit one with the rarer Type A specs that included more horsepower. This is actually one of three Daytonas that Micholotti rebodied, the other two being more slab-shaped and, in the eyes of many, far inferior to the styling of our Corvette-styled car, another of the NART Spyders. "NART," of course, being the initials of the North American Racing Team, under whose name Luigi, Jr., did everything.

Given the choice, most racers would want a coupe because it has a more rigid body than an open car. At least this open car had a targa-style top with a removable roof hatch. It also had an electrically operated rear window.

The car made its debut as a Michelotti design at the Geneva Auto Salon in 1974, where maybe Michelotti was hoping Ferrari would choose to keep that chassis going with a new exterior design. Those hopes were in vain, as Ferrari would push the mid-engine Boxer, relegating the front-engined Daytona to history.

FIRST TRY AT RACING

Apparently, the only buyer for the car after the Geneve Salon was Dan Ward, an American with money and the itch to go racing, and where else to start your racing career but at the top, at the 24 Heures du Mans? I thought, to hear Dan tell it, he was a driver, but the old entry list says the scheduled drivers were Jean Pierre Malcher and Patrick Langlois. Dan Ward is listed over on the sponsor side, as "Ward/NART." Of course, having been a sponsor at LeMans is, how you say, not a bad tidbit to drop at the next Ferrari Owner's Club meeting, don'tcha know.

Luigi Chinetti's NART team entered it alongside three other Ferraris: a standard Competition Daytona (Group 4); a heavily modified 308GT/4; and a near standard 365GT/4 BB—a first-series Boxer making its debut at the Sarthe.

The Daytona Spyder had what is referred to as a GP IV Series 3 engine, prepared in Modena for NART, with high-lift cams, racing headers, a higher compression ratio, and special racing side-mounted exhaust. It was also fitted with a huge, 70-liter fuel tank. With only a short time to prepare the car, it seems mechanics looked at another 365GTB/4 Group IV works car that was in the shop, No. 15685, and thought, here's a way to save time, and took the 478-horsepower engine out of the coupe and put it in the spyder.

There are reports that it ran faster on the top end than the Competition Daytona coupes, with their Pininfarina design and coachwork.

POLITICS INTERVENE

But Italians being Italian, and Frenchmen being French, and Americans being feistier than the preceding two put together, there was many a slip twixt the cup and the lip and, after the NART team's 308GT/4 was not accepted as a production car, there were further arguments about who had been chosen as drivers (nationalities the unspoken issue here), and NART withdrew all their cars only 88 minutes before the starting flag dropped and left for America.

THE SECOND TRY AT BIG-TIME RACING

The NART contingent then returned to New York, and 15965 officially went to Dan Ward. Three years later, it was entered by Otto Zipper (no, not related to Eric Von Zipper...), a Ferrari dealer in Los Angeles, in the 1978 Daytona 24-hour race.

Drivers were scheduled to be Dan Devendorf-Kline and Michael Keyser. The head mechanic was my old Ferrari mechanic, Bruno Borri, of Modena Imports in Los Angeles. Now I wish I could tell a happy story here, but damn if history didn't repeat itself. The car was all prepped for the race, but withdrawn after a protest by (eventual overall race winner) Peter Gregg, driver of a Porsche Turbo, on the grounds of its non-standard body.

So it was that this race car—developed by a team that had won LeMans only a few years earlier, and designed by one of the most respected coachbuilders in Italy—eventually ended up as just another car flying a balloon on a used car lot in West Los Angeles. Well, to be honest it wasn't just *any* used car lot, but one full of exotic cars, called The VIP Toy Store, in Los Angeles. By then, the white paint job had been repainted your usual Ferrari used-car color of Rosso Corsa and the racing interior was replaced by tan leather, all hints of race-car life evaporated.

CONVERSION TO STREET CAR

The next owner, in the late '70s, was a famous name in car collecting circles: John Mecom, of Texas, an oil man and race car sponsor who back in the '60s, bought seemingly one of everything—even cars whose makers were competing with each other.

He decided he wanted the Chinetti/Michellotti Daytona to be a street car and spent a bunch more money converting it.

According to *Thoroughbred and Classic Car* magazine in England, in '86 it was offered by Steve Forristall's G.T. Cars in Texas, but the only price this writer could find was a January, 1988, price when it went across the block in Scottsdale for $370,000.

It might have been Patrick Ryan who bought it in Scottsdale. One significant moment he had with the car, besides racing it in vintage events, was having Old Man Chinetti tell him at an Atlanta show what really happened at LeMans—why the car didn't make the race. I would have loved to have been a fly on the wall then, as politics at LeMans is always world-class gossip.

BACK TO THE LEMANS SPECS

In 2001, it was sold at auction by Christies for $295,000 from the Patrick Ryan estate. By the way, in the catalog description, they don't say if it ever got the engine back that it was built with. Ironically, you could say the borrowed coupe's engine is more historical because that's what was used in practice at LeMans.

In 2005, the car was offered for sale by Jean Guikas' GTC, a classic car dealer in Marseille.

By 2006, you might think the car could rest on its laurels as a one-time entrant in two major 24-hour races. But no, because of vintage racing and its high demand for exotic cars with even tenuous connections to real races of the past, the Chinetti/Michellotti Daytona went back to racing. Its new owner entered it in the European Ferrari Challenge, the 2007 Tour Auto, and the US Ferrari Challenge Laguna Seca, where it won its class. But as a street car, it was not exciting enough, so it was converted back to its original Le Mans specifications and, in 2008, the car was entered in the Classic LeMans, where it actually got to run on the very same track it was built to race on almost a quarter century earlier.

After that went to a Swiss owner, who has taken it to almost every significant world-class Ferrari event.

Its significance is that, although Ferrari built several Competition Daytona Coupes, this is the only Competition NART Daytona Spyder ever built. Technically, it was not built as a Spyder by Ferrari but was converted by an authorized (in that Ferrari themselves had previously commissioned Michelotti to body cars) coachbuilder—and it was converted from Coupe to Spyder "in period," i.e. when the Daytona Coupe was still in production.

So, you could say this car indeed had a checkered career but has come back, making up for those two big slaps in the face back in the '70s.

Maybe some of you even rejected it because you thought a Daytona should look like what Pininfarina wrought.

Present value? I'd have to say, writing this in 2016, one would start at $2 million or at least a million more than a box-stock 365GTB/4 Daytona Coupe.

After all, there is only one NART Daytona Spyder.

Lesson to be learned? When a car is successful on a race track, it's a little difficult to get a bargain on it, because the cafe racers like to tool around on the street in a car "that raced at such-and-such." (You can just see yourself saying "Well, down the Mulsanne straight at LeMans, it clocked 190 mph...")

Now this car, technically, qualified for two world-class 24-

hour races but was doomed from running either by the nastiest sort of backroom politics. But I would venture to say that the right time to buy it was: right after it failed to make LeMans; or right after it got kicked off the grid at Daytona. Or heck, even when it was on the used-car lots of the greater Los Angeles area. So, in essence, if you want a deal, don't waste time trying to outbid others to buy the winner. Instead, I say go for the loser, because now, with its status as a unique NART Spyder, it is a winner again.

Chapter 42
Now You See It, Now You Don't
(1960 Corvette XP700)
Is it really gone?

Back in the '60s, I used to know a guy in Detroit who was a top-drawer exec for GM—head of styling, in fact. And when he replaced the founder of GM Styling, Mr. Harley Earl, Bill Mitchell had to fill some pretty big boots.

Like his predecessor, Mitchell was a snappy dresser (that's actually what they called it back then, "snappy"), and in the summer he sported white suits, panama hats, and two-tone shoes. He may have been rotund, but he was a well-dressed rotund.

He also liked to have dream cars built and use them as his own personal car at times. Earl had initiated that particular executive perk at GM with the LeSabre dream car—a car that reportedly cost more than a million to build. For his first dream car, I kind of think Mitchell did it on his own nickel; it's a red Corvette with some Euro styling, He added an oval grille that looks like it's from an OSCA. At that time he was still Earl's underling; you can just see him thinking: "I'll show the old man that I can originate dream cars, too."

Hey, his ploy worked. The car was taken in-house by Earl and given a much fancier re-do for its role as an official GM show car)

It was repainted silver, chrome surrounds added here and there, the upholstery became silver leather, the roof got a double-bubble canopy with a tank periscope between the two bubbles to see rearward. Along the spine between the two bubbles were ventilation louvers.

The car was re-named the XP-700, XP for "Experimental project" or some such mumbo-jumbo. I suspect the guys in Styling liked to pretend they were doing secret stuff, like developing future flying craft, and actually some of them were in

the military during the war(s) (both WWII and Korea) and did in fact shape some Allied weapons. Mitchell himself worked on aircraft instrumentation design. So, even after the war, they liked to be mysterious about their secret stuff. The ostensible purpose of the XP-700 was to give Corvette fans a preview of the upcoming 1961 Corvette with the ducktail upswept rear. Some say the elliptical grille cavity strongly resembled that of a one-off Ferrari 250GT by Pininfarina and, it's true, there was such a car built in Italy.

You would think Pininfarina would yelp that GM was stealing their design cues but since GM was the Big Dog in the automotive world it was more like Pininfarina was always nibbling around the edges hoping for a GM contract, which they got in doing some Cadillac Broughams)

The front hood also had big flush deck hot air release vents. I am proud to say Pininfarina stole those decades later for the GTC/4 Ferrari. Usually, GM is accused of copying the Euros, but this was a case wherein GM had it first.

The car also had wire wheels. Mitchell loved wire wheels. He put wire wheels on almost every concept car Styling built for awhile, at least until real racers switched to magnesium wheels, a trend he reluctantly followed.

The plexiglass bubble top seems like it would be hell on a hot day, but it was sprayed with a metal coating that was see-through, like mirrored sunglasses, so wasn't that hot. I was ready to credit Mitchell, or maybe Larry Shinoda, a California hot rodder Mitchell had hired as his "private designer" for this until I read that the bubble top was inspired by the '55 Lancia Aurelia 2500 GT Rayon d'Azur, (referred to on one website as the GT2500 Nardi Vignale) , a one-off which had the same bubble roof except that the air intake between the two bubbles on that car was just an air scoop, not a periscope.

MY RIDE

The Corvette Mako Shark also had a double bubble top, but a body style more reminiscent of the future Corvette Stingray roadster. One day, back in the mid-'60s, I was over at the Tech Center in Warren, Michigan, having lunch with Bill, and he asked me if I wanted to go for a ride in it. Would I? That's like asking a Cessna pilot would he like to fly around a bit in a SR-71 Blackbird!

As we toodled about the grounds, I was admiring things like the black crackle finish to the dash (from racing Ferraris) and the wood-rimmed Nardi polished-alloy spoke steering wheel (a present from Enzo Ferrari) and the stopwatch on the console so you could impress your passenger with your 0-60 time, an idea he cribbed from what Ferrari did on some very special VIP cars like the 410 and 400SA.

THE RUSE

Until that ride, I had assumed that the Mitchell red custom begat the XP-700 and that in turn begat the Mako Shark (later called the Mako Shark I when the Mako Shark II came along). But, as we were riding along, Mitchell said, "We built this atop the XP-700 because the brass windshield frame would cost too much to do all over again."

Mark Jordan, is the son of a later GM VP in Charge of Styling. He was lucky enough to drive the Mako Shark I around during his high school days, and confirmed to me that the XP-700 was underneath the Mako Shark I.

But I'm a reporter. Pictures stick in my brain. I dimly remember seeing a picture somewhere of Mitchell with the two cars -- the Mako Shark and the XP700—parked side by side. Now it may be that one of the cars was just a painstakingly well-finished clay model. Or maybe the photo was "photoshopped" (or whatever they called it before Photoshop was invented, maybe "airbrushing").

THE REVELATION

But I regained hope on 9-9-16 after I had begun fact checking this book before it went to press. I dutifully wrote the lead GM Historian and asked him what's the deal on the XP-700— is it underneath the Mako Shark I or not? I was surprised when he wrote back confirming that this picture shows they both co-existed at the same time, so the Mako Shark I is not built atop the XP-700. And he sent a picture that shows them side-by-side during a show and tell event being conducted by Mitchell.

My old friend Bill conned me!

The GM historian, Christo Datini, said: "Please find attached a number of documents that provide evidence of the XP-700 existing after the completion of the XP-755 Shark (aka Mako Shark I.

Styling memos from March 1961 confirm that while it was originally the plan to use the XP-700 chassis for the basis of the XP-755, this ultimately did not happen. The attached photograph dated August 1, 1962 shows both cars in the background. The Styling work order summary for XP-700 indicates that the running car existed at least until December 31, 1962 and even though plans had been made earlier to use some of its components for XP-755 Shark.

The work order summary for XP-755 indicates that Mitchell requested a Corvette running car from a production chassis with a double bubble hardtop, 'ala XP-700.' In October of 1962, Mitchell was informed by Chevrolet that in order to install a new 1963 Corvette rear suspension on the XP-755, a whole new chassis would be required. Thus it remained a solid axle car.

As for when the XP-700 was scrapped, we have no documentation to confirm. The tooling appears to have been scrapped per an order of October 1964 (attached) but no memo mentions that scrapping of the running car."

Was it scrapped? There is an ominous clue. On the website, *Corvette Forum*, the Fall 2014 report called "On Solid Ground, Bloomington 2014 in Pictures," there is a picture of the front clip of two feet or so of the XP700, including all of the unique trim. Below that picture is a caption that says the piece was reportedly found after long storage in a Michigan home. There was no price on it and the photographer says he didn't ask because of the old saying: "If you have to ask, you can't afford it." Well, this reminds me of the times when airliners crash and they can't find a clue of its fate until a piece of debris floats up on a beach somewhere. If this piece is the real nose of the XP-700 that could mean that car is a goner…

So, score one for the barn finders. There's a possibility that the XP-700 lives, and that someday I will discover it, with a nice coat of patina, in a barn somewhere in Oakland County, Michigan, (though maybe without that nose that was offered at that swap meet…)

Chapter 43
Orphans in a Storm
(1964 Pontiac XP-833 Banshee)
Sometimes, even a prototype can't find love...

Imagine a hand-built prototype from a major automaker popping up on eBay? Hey, it happens.

This is the story of two cars—which are, indeed, documented Detroit factory prototypes—in which the purchase of one as a quick turnaround investment proved troublesome. Herein lies a cautionary tale.

Called Project XP-833, and dating back to 1964, the XP-833 Banshees—a coupe and a companion convertible—were done at the request of the celebrated (and later vilified by a government-launched "sting" dope deal he fell for) executive John DeLorean, who once headed up Pontiac Motor Division. The Banshee was envisioned as a mid-price model that would slot in between Chevrolet's Corvette and Camaro (and Pontiac's upcoming Firebird). Like the Corvette, it had a two-seat fiber-

glass body. One website in Holland says that the target retail price was to have been an incredibly low $2500 (presumably for the inline-six-powered base model), which would have underpriced the Corvette.

It had the long hood/short rear deck of a European sports car, and looked far sleeker than the Corvette—and had to be at least 500 pounds lighter with the six-cylinder. It was built on a 90-inch-wheelbase, freshly designed, steel platform chassis, the already existing A-body perimeter frame deemed far too heavy for sport use. Pontiac fans say to credit the body design to PMD designer Jack Humbert under Chuck Jordan's corporate design leadership. Everyone who knows GM postwar design history knows that Jordan was the Ferrari fan at the Tech Center, so we can surmise that's where the Ferrari influence came from.

Similar to the Ford GT, the Banshee had fixed seats with movable pedals. Two complete, running prototypes were built; decades later they began appearing on the occasional auction block.

Under the hood of the coupe was an inline six based on a Chevrolet block, boasting an oh-so-European single-overhead-camshaft, cross-flow cylinder head. Sadly, it was the 155-horsepower version with the single-barrel carb; Pontiac later offered a Firebird with a 215-horsepower version, called the "Sprint," that had a four-barrel. No one can say why the coupe didn't have the hotter six, or even the V-8 they put in the prototype roadster.

Perhaps DeLorean was treading softly, as there was a big anti-performance faction among leadership at GM. Maybe it was a "soft" proposal, designed to lure the top brass into approving it. Then, once he got the Banshee into production, he'd slip in the V-8 he had already determined would fit in the open car.

DE LOREAN VIEWED WITH SUSPICION FROM TOP FLOOR

DeLorean was a notorious trickster. Earlier in his career, he had slipped a bigger V-8 into the Tempest than allowed by corporation rules, inaugurating the muscle-car era with the fabled GTO (thumbed his nose at GM brass *and* stole the name of Ferrari's hottest GT car!). When the suits found out, they said, Okay, but you can only make 1000. Well, 50,000 or so GTOs later, the brass made nary a peep.

So, maybe DeLorean's reputation preceded him. Neither Banshee got approved.

With the six-cylinder tuned to produce 165 horsepower, the Banshee, with a curb weight of 2,286 pounds, would have been a barnstormer.

But it didn't get slated for production. Why? Difficult to say, now that so much water has gone under the bridge. One reason might have been the empire builders within GM who felt it threatened their turf. Especially the powerful "Father of the Corvette," Zora Arkus-Duntov (he should more properly be called the stepfather of the Corvette, because he was hired at GM in 1955—after the Corvette was already in production). He didn't want DeLorean's Banshees undermining his Corvette empire.

One difference between DeLorean and Duntov is that De-Lorean had heard of cars like the Ferrari GTO and races like the 24 Hours of LeMans. Duntov, by contrast, had actually *raced* at LeMans (in '55, for Porsche), making him GM's leading expert in what makes a European-type car. Duntov didn't like anyone at GM who said they were a bigger expert in European race cars than him.

SOLD TO EMPLOYEES

The Banshee was shot down in 1966. The story of what happened to the Banshees after that treads a familiar path: both were ordered destroyed; both were sold instead to employees close to the project. The coupe seen on eBay was first sold directly by GM to a private individual and stayed in that family all the way until 2006, when it was consigned to a Barrett-Jackson auction, where a Pontiac collector named Len Napoli bought it. He looked at it as an investment. Lenny Napoli owns a business, Napoli Classic Cars in Milford, Connecticut, and specializes in Pontiac GTOs.

You can't blame Napoli for paying over $210,600 for it when he saw the coupe pop up at the 35th Barrett-Jackson auction. A year earlier, at the same auction firm's 2005 Scottsdale sale, another concept from GM, the 1954 Oldsmobile F-88, had sold for several million. Napoli thought that sale was proof positive that factory prototypes were now as good as gold.

"When I saw it come up, I didn't think I was going to be able to buy it, because the prices that year were, like, insane," Mr. Napoli said in a telephone interview with The New York Times.

He bought the Banshee coupe and sought to turn it around. But, in subsequent auctions, he couldn't sell it and had to resort to eBay, where he listed it at a buy-it-now price of $750,000.

Napoli told the NY Times that its past bid history "offers no reflection of the car's true value," and that "the Banshee's next owner is just a mouse click away." He added, "I have just got to get the right person who wants a museum piece," he said.

The Bortz Auto Collection was owner of the more seldom-seen convertible for a time, but that, too, was listed for sale on eBay.

At this writing, it's unclear to this writer where the two orphaned Banshees are now.

Ironically, all the effort by GM engineers and designers to create the Banshee wasn't totally wasted, if you take the long view. When the 1968 Corvette was revealed, guess what? Same lines. The designers of the Opel GT over in Germany must have paid very close attention to it. And can we say the success of the Pontiac Solstice was not influenced by the two Banshees? (Indicative of the Universe's "quirky" sense of humor, the Solstice and its Saturn Sky sister were both successful, while the GM divisions that sold them were not). All those cars proved there was a market for small roadsters with sexy styling.

Lesson to be learned? Not every concept car from an automaker is automatically a solid-gold investment. Especially if it wasn't shown around much at auto shows. The Banshees appear to be in that more mysterious category of what are called "internal concepts"–cars built for management review, as opposed to one-off cars intended to be stars of the auto shows and which were seen and lusted after by millions.

Plus the six-cylinder concept was proposed when V-8s still ruled the roost.

And one thing a buyer of either of these cars can't count on is Pontiac renting or leasing their historic prototype show car from you to show with their new models. Not like those lucky collectors who get calls from firms like Bugatti and Mercedes and Jaguar asking if they would mind bringing their old classics to new-car unveilings. GM's Pontiac division was summarily thrown into the dustbin of history, so Pontiac lovers have to suck it up and continue the visibility of the brand all by their lonesome.

In a way, when the automaker dies, you might say that a little bit of the appeal of their prototypes dies with them.

The coupe appeared at the Mecum sale in Monterey in 2010, but did not sell at $325,000. Right weekend, right event, but the cars had too little visibility originally to be much lusted after today.

But hope springs eternal. The Banshees could be future concours/auction superstars. Maybe if presented with more documentation, such as pictures of DeLorean with the cars or a display of beaucoup internal correspondence regarding his ambitious plans.

And it could also depend on how well other Detroit prototypes sell for—if one, say, cracks the $4-million-dollar barrier, well, maybe that will make more investors think they got what stockholders call "upside potential."

Yeah, and pigs can fly...

Chapter 44
The Shah's Chrysler and Its Missing Twin (1957 Chrysler 300C)
The Shah had a lotta toys. This one mystifies every one...

Now everybody knows the late Shah of Iran was a real, bona-fide car enthusiast. Like having a Lamborghini Miura made up to look like a one-off race car (see the Shah Miura in Incredible Barn Finds No. 2). The Shah owned over 1,000 cars.

Well, the Shah eventually left Iran for medical reasons but never returned and a government agency glommed onto the collection. Unfortunately, some of the cars were stolen and/or destroyed but, I am happy to report, some of the cars survived and are now being restored and displayed.

The car I covet most in his collection is the Bizzarrini GT 5300, but I wouldn't turn down a Rolls PV if he had one by James Young. I don't think the cars are for sale, though. They're hoping someday tourists will want to see the collection. Anyway, the car that's a mystery is the huge Chrysler 375 (some say

CHRYSLER 300

300). It is a beautiful copper color and built by Ghia.

Did Chrysler initiate this car? I think Ghia did it all by themselves, with no input from the U.S. (though, of course, the US was promoting the Shah at that time; some say the U.S. engineered him being put on the throne in the first place).

In researching the car, I found Ghia drawings. But the deeper I got into it, the more confused I got, so I'm afraid I am left to hope that some longtime Chrysler 300 expert and/or Ghia expert might know the answer. George F. Kotarba of the Netherlands has researched the car, and says it is a 1957 Chrysler-Ghia 300 (chassis number 3N551511; engine number 3NE551550). He says the car was owned by the late Empress of Iran, Soraya Esfandiary-Bakhtiari.

The car has huge tailfins, which makes me think Chrysler was involved. I don't think Ghia was into tailfins that much. I wonder if Virgil Exner, Sr., did this car on the side; maybe someone in the State department said, Hey, our buddy in Iran wants a big ol' Chrysler bodied by Ghia, got any ideas?

Okay, so far it seems pretty straightforward. Now I will throw in a couple curves. There's also a car called the Chrysler Special. It looks similar, only not so damn long and jacked out of proportion as the Shah's car. But that could be one of Gene Casaroll's (owner of Dual Motors) prototypes, built before he made the production four-seat convertible Dual-Ghias. That car was displayed at a WPC Chrysler meet in California in 2009.

Now to muddy the waters further, on the AACA website is the following letter by Virgil Exner, Jr., whom I have met and who is a very witty guy and astute observer of the whole Chrysler-Ghia relationship:

Dear Mr. Kotarba,

It has come to my attention that you are looking into a Ghia built Chrysler 300.

"My father did not do the whole design or the renderings for the 300 in question. It certainly was someone connected

with Ghia. The renderings were probably done by either Tom Tjaarda, Filipo Sapino, or Sergio Sartorelli.

Ghia did many of these 'custom cars' using soft tooling from having built the Chrysler Specials (several), the Chrysler GS I (a low volume of 23 or 24), the Chrysler Falcon, the Dual Ghia, production parts, etc. They were largely contracted for and sold by Charles LaDouche, the main Chrysler distributor in Paris. They were built with Chrysler's and my father's blessing."

This all makes sense. So, according to his son, it wasn't Exner, Sr., involved in the 375, but the Chrysler distributor in Paris, who also put a series of Chrysler Specials into production. And everyone knows the Shah was a big Francophile (in fact one of the things he did to grease the skids under his regime was throw a huge party where everything including the food was flown in from Paris, which ticked off the Iranians, who felt insulted that nothing Persian was to be found at the Shah's big party).

THE OTHER 375

But as I pursued my inquiries I got word there is another 375, one in America, green with white.I am told Valerio Moretti's book, "Ghia," shows both cars on the same page.

By the way, the reason they are not called 300s is because these particular cars were named in reference to their horsepower ratings. The '55 300-based Ghia 300 had 300 HP. The '57 300C-based Ghia 375 had 375 HP. Other names used on cars from Ghia had marketing connections, like "Thomas Special," "Shah of Persia," "GS-1" (a short production series of Thomas Special-like models), and "Chrysler Specials" (a minor variation of the GS-1).

So there it is, Ghia fans. As a result of my research, I now know there are two Ghia 375s, one in Iran, one in California. I would love to know where and when the one in California was found (perhaps bought out of a museum) and what was paid for it at the time. The one in Iran, well, they say their cars are not for sale, and, as a keeper of the flame, I hope they make it to having a museum. I am always a fan of those mega-collectors who had an eye for what was good and who even instigated the design and building of some very special cars.

Lesson learned? Sometimes you start down one path of inquiry, hoppin' down the bunny trail so to speak, expecting to find one thing and *BAM* you find another of equal interest. I started out looking for how the Shah's Chrysler 375 came to be and ended up finding there's been a similar car sighted in California. So that California car is going on my list of "possibles." There's only 33 million people in California, I just have to narrow it down. But, hey, knowing it's in the Golden State gives me a place to start.

Chapter 45
The Return of the Native: The Bertone Spicup (1972 BMW 2800)
Hidden in Plain Sight...

One rule of the auto industry, carved in stone by legal staffs, is "Thou shall not sell prototypes."

People who believe that are also shopping for a bridge in Brooklyn.

This one, the BMW Spicup, is an unusual car: a coupe with a retractable roof. It was built by the design house of Carrzzeria Bertone from the hand of the same designer who did the Miura, the Stratos, and the Countach, Marcello Gandini. It was basically an attempt to showcase Bertone's concept of how a roof could be stowed easily. It was seen as controversial at the time, maybe so much so that it did not spawn a production model.

Gandini used a BMW 2500 chassis as the Spicup's foundation, though the chassis had to be shortened for the new body.

An all-new dashboard was designed, using regular BMW gauges. Plus there were new seats and carpeting, in a somewhat bilious combination of two-tone, green-on-green upholstery.

Bertone bragged about its automatic top, but the only car this writer can remember with an automatic targa top was the home-market Japanese version of the Honda Del Sol decades

ago. The engine in the Spicup was not from a 2500 but from the BMW 2800, a 2.8-liter, six-cylinder engine which cranked out 170 bhp. It was coupled to a four-speed manual, so this was one prototype that was fully drivable, unlike the many "push-mobiles," only able to hobble up onto a show stage with the aid of an internal electric motor.

The car came out not many years after the Alfa Romeo Montreal, and had similar semi-hidden "eyelid" headlight covers with motorized lids.

The strong BMW part was the famous "double kidney" grille motif. Although the kidneys seemed to be stuffed with something that looks in pictures like leather pillows!

SOLD DOWN THE RIVER TO A DEALER

Though BMW has a museum, they didn't see keeping the Spicup around after its lukewarm reception, so they sold it on down the road. One report is that, in the mid-'70s, it was offered at Auto-Becker (Duesseldorf, Germany),one of the biggest car dealers in Europe. One website report has someone trading in an Iso-Rivolta (Bertone body, Chevrolet V-8 engine) for the Spicup; maybe the dealer thought he got the better part of the deal, since the Iso was at least a known entity.

The first private owner, a Dutchman (or, as another rumor has it, a pair of brothers),put 60,000 miles (100,000 kms) on it in the Netherlands. That owner didn't have much respect for its originality and painted it orange. Furthermore, though it originally had a separate engine cover, that cover was attached by the owner(s?) to the hood so it didn't lift separately (originally it was similar to the Pontiac Trans-Am where the hood had a hole through which the air scoop projected).

After several decades in the barn (maybe literally and not just figuratively), another Dutch buyer, Paul Koot, bought it in a two-car deal that included something called an Intermeccanica Indra in 2008. Roland D'Ieteren, a Belgian restorer, brought the car back to its original livery and it was well received at the 2009 Villa d'Este Concours, where, coincidentally, BMW was the acting sponsor. The irony being BMW originally thinking it a memory not worth keeping.

As one forum poster on Retrorides.Proboards.com said, "The fact that the brothers used a one off concept car (albeit with production mechanicals) as a daily driver is the icing on the cake. Most show cars get forgotten and barely driven even if they're runners. The Spicup was displayed, abandoned, redis-covered, rejuvenated, used every day, forgotten again and finally restored."

This writer says Hooray! It is proof that some treasures are sometimes hidden in plain sight.

Lessons to be learned: Prototypes do come up for sale. Espe-cially if they are unloved at the time they are born. Even ugly children can grow up to be beautiful. Regardless of some detail design gaffs (why Gandini thought the '57 Mercury Turnpike Cruiser rear window was worth copying is a mystery), the fact remains this car is historically significant, a combination of Gandini in mid-career, Bertone at their best in craftsmanship on the bodywork, and German engineering on the mechanicals.

Not many concept cars have been driven so hard, treated so cavalierly, and gone on to star again at concours d'elegance. Kudos to the buyers who first recognized its specialness; and thanks to Paul Koot for bringing it back to its present glory. And kudos to BMW for offering new support and recognition for a car that they had once cast from their midst.

Chapter 46
The See-Through Lambo
(1967 Lamborghini Marzal)
Hey, ladies, it helps if you have nice legs...

Road & Track, in describing this concept car, said, "A Bertone design so fresh that everything else looks old fashioned," in its July, 1967, report on the stunning Lamborghini Marzal show car.

Introduced at the Geneva Motor Show only four months earlier, the P200 Marzal was the result of a close collaboration between Bertone and Lamborghini.

Ferrucio Lamborghini was a bit different than Enzo Ferrari. Right from the beginning, Lamborghini wanted only to build road cars, not race cars. Ferrari built road cars only to finance the building and racing of race cars. Ferrucio thought of racing as a way to pour money down the sewer. You might as well pour oil on yourself and tear up the dollar bills.

The Marzal was created by Lamborghini to explore the idea of a car that could offer comfortable seating for four, but still be high performance.

Like other Lambos (including the Miura), it was named for a strain of fighting bull, the Marzal.

The only letdown the wild design has is when you lift the rear engine access hood and find not a V-12 like the Miura or previous P400, but an in-line six–basically the rear bank of a Miura's 3,929cc V-12, fed by horizontal Weber carburetors and mated to the standard five-speed transmission.

That engine was rated at 175 bhp which, I hafta tell you, does not sound like a horsepower figure I would associate with cars bearing the badge of the prancing bull.

The engine had to be turned 180 degrees compared to the Miura's layout so that it was behind the rear axle, therefore making it more of a rear-engine car than a mid-engine car. That packaging made the car roomier for four people, but you have to wonder about handling disadvantages of a rear-engine car.

The radiator was also at the rear, which meant passengers could put their luggage up front, the load area sharing 11 cubic feet of loading space with the 21-gallon fuel tank.

The chassis, as hard as it is to believe, is a heavily-modified Miura chassis, its wheelbase extended by 120mm to be able to fit those extra two passengers.

The designer was the one-man-band (because he did all the work himself), Marcello Gandini. He chose to use long gull-wing doors, which alone would have given the car a distinctive look, but he went a step or three further and used long, *see-through* gullwing doors.

Of course, the glass all had to be made specially made. This was done by the Belgian company, Glaverbel.

The rumor is that Ferruccio Lamborghini objected to those doors, showing the area beneath the waistline which would offer, egad, a glimpse of a lady's legs. Evidentally he lost out, and the car is ever the more memorable for it.

Modesty prevails with respect to views from behind, though. There is no rear window, its position occupied by a panel made of aluminum slats riveted together.

The wild exterior is matched by an equally wild interior,

which goes heavy on the hexagonal honeycomb theme with the dashboard and center console that housed most controls. The hexagons carry over to the seat's cushions and backrests.

The car didn't stay static to the way it was first presented, undergoing some "in period" variations to details like the steering wheel, gear knob, instruments, and trim.

The Marzal's Campagnolo magnesium wheels echoed those of the Miura but with that hexagonal theme.

The lean, pointed nose featured six Marchal quartz-iodine headlamps. The body was steel, though, thankfully, the massive front bonnet was aluminum.

Gandini had another reason to make this car more distinctive than any other he had done: he had become Bertone's leading designer after Giorgetto Giugiaro left, and, where previous Bertone cars had Giugiaro roots, like the Miura, Montreal, and Fiat Dino Coupe to name three, the Marzal was all Gandini.

Now, some show cars are naught but "pushmobiles," having a small electric motor to drive them onto and off of stages at auto shows, but this car was fully drivable. In fact, Prince Rainier made an appearance in it at the Monaco Grand Prix on May 7, 1967, toodling around the circuit with Princess Grace.

Not long after that, editors of the Italian magazine *Quattroruote* drove it and commented that it was a spirited performer in their October, 1967, issue. Although never fully developed as a production car, the Marzal was estimated to be good for 140 mph. Had the car gone into production, that top speed would have needed to be increased to 160 mph to live up to the Lamborghini legend.

But the Marzal was not produced. A year after its introduction, though, the Lamborghini Espada four-seat production coupe was introduced—thankfully with a V-12 but, alas, not having the rear-engine layout and glass doors. The doors almost made it—the prototypes had gullwing doors—but they disappeared by the time the car reached production.

The fact that the Espada remained in production all the way

to 1978 demonstrated how well it filled a niche Ferrari wasn't aiming at.

Among the comments paid to the car was one by the esteemed British journalist LJK Setright, who described it as "perhaps the most extravagant piece of virtuoso styling to have come out of Europe since the war."

Bertone would like to have kept it in its museum, but a series of bad business moves forced Bertone into bankruptcy, and this car was one of six Bertone prototypes sold at auction in 2011. It was sold on Saturday, May 21, 2011, for 1,512,000 Euros, over two million dollars at the time.

Lesson learned? Carrozzerias do sell prototypes. This one seems to be "well bought" because it is a drivable car that could be taken on a tour like the Colorado Grand. It wasn't a bargain, but it's got a lot of plusses going for it, like being created during the time Ferrucio was still in charge (as important as buying a Ferrari that was created when Enzo was running his Ferrari firm), and being a one-off car that inspired a production car.

But was it a barn find? I say a qualified "yes," the qualifier being what it goes for the next time it comes up for auction. I'd say that, since Audi bought Lamborghini, the firm is no longer struggling. There will be plenty of future opportunities for vintage Lambos to be highlighted, thus this car will be much sought after in the future, unlike the cars representing brands that have disappeared from the face of the earth.

Chapter 47
The French BMW 507 (1957 BMW 507)
Was it ever available cheap?

Now it may come as a surprise to some that one of the places to find a barn find treasure is at a museum.

Especially if it's not a car museum. Now why would a non-car museum have a treasured car?

Well, let's put it this way. When a generous individual wants to give something, make a bequest of some object or property, if you are the beneficiary, in this case the Museum, it's best not to object. No, sir. You take it and figure out what to do with it later.

So it was back in 1962 when the French-born designer Raymond Loewy, whose career was mainly in America, decided to give his custom-designed French-bodied BMW 507 to a museum called the Museum of Natural History in Los Angeles. This was a museum with dinosaurs and other "natural" things. But they had already been donated a bunch of cars, and took the Loewy car in and it wasn't until decades later that the public saw the car as it was loaned to a newer museum in town, called

the Petersen Museum, founded by a donation of funds from Robert E. Petersen, founder of a magazine empire (*Hot Rod, Motor Trend*, etc.).

An article in *Los Angeles* magazine in 2000 said that the Petersen museum was started as an offshoot of the Natural History Museum, to house the cars. But the academics in charge of the Natural History museum weren't car people so it was inevitable that the Petersen eventually went off on its own.

Some will argue that Loewy was not a car designer per se, no, they say, he was really an "industrial designer." He designed lots of things, such as more modern exteriors for steam locomotives and steamships, airplane interiors, furniture, and the like. He is most famous for the Studebaker Avanti, but if you look into it more, he had several one-off cars built to show off his design talents, most of them bodied by his favorite firm, a small French coachbuilder named Pichon et Parat. His idea with these one-off cars was to drum up business, and if he didn't get commissions to design cars, he would sell the car.

The three most notable of his one-off cars were the Lancia Loraymo, this 507, and an E-type which eventually reached another owner and sold at auction. Now some of his detractors will say Loewy was more of a "design boss" with underlings doing the design, people like Virgil Exner Jr., Bob Bourke, and others who would submit sketches and the boss would choose one to give to the coachbuilder. I say, in his defense, Loewy had the design sensitivity to choose the design direction and the designs are still to be credited to him.

If this car resembles his later Studebaker Avanti, it is no accident, though it was done earlier. Some of the similar ideas that were re-used on the Avanti were the large backlight, the bladed front fenders , the integrated turn indicators, door cuts into the roofline, and the egg-shaped wheel openings. But on the 507 they were more startling because the car was so much different than the 507 with removable hardtop that BMW released into production.

French Pichon and Parat de Sens built the car with the then

futuristic idea of having a rigid cell surrounded byzones of absorption. It is bodied in Duralinos, and equipped with a windshield which the French describe as " double curvature." One part of the design that has, alas, not weathered the decades was the horizontal taillights combined with bumpers that projected easily a foot out from the body. While they gave the body a clean shape, they would have broken the taillights on impact so it was silly to combine the two.

The car was exhibited at the Salon in Paris in 1957. There are, of course, some who feel that the BMW 507 was just fine the way Count Albrecht von Goertz designed it for production.

There was a link between the two designers.

Like Loewy, Albrecht von Goertz also was an immigrant who made his career as a designer in America. He was a son of a German aristocrat (his full name: Albrecht Graf von Schlitz gen. von Görtz und von Wrisberg). He left Germany before the war, while his Jewish mother was later deported to Theresienstadt . He had started out life in America doing repairs on cars but by 1939 showed his first car, a hand-made concept car based upon a Mercury. That car was presented at the NY World Exhibition in 1939.

During the war Goertz enlisted the US Army, and served in the Pacific (1940-1945), then postwar, studied at Pratt Institute; it was there that he then drew the attention of Loewy who later hired Goertz to work for him at Studebaker. In 1953 Goertz established himself in New York as an independent designer and it was at the instigation of the BMW American importer that he designed what became two legendary BMWs --the BMW 503 and BMW 507, both cars breaking the idea that BMW cars should be small but alas, both sold poorly because of the exchange rate, and were too high priced for the U.S. market.

One wonders if one reason Loewy chose the 507 was because his former student had designed the production version; was it a way to show the world that his student was "still" a student compared to the master? To put the Count in his place, so to speak?

Before going to press, I tried to check on the status of this car. I know the Petersen shows it but I can't say for sure the Museum of Natural History doesn't still own it.

So here's another case where a little research might pay off. Find out who owns it and write a check (just send them the photocopy). BMW has shown interest in former cars they built, as witness their restoration of the "first" Elvis BMW.

That's the lesson to be learned here—that just because a car is in a Museum doesn't mean it will be there forever—Museums have different missions and the more a car's presence there is in contradiction to their mission, the more amenable the Museum Board might be to selling it.

Hey, it's worth a try….oh, by the way, I'd say now that even regular 507 roadsters are bringing in over one million dollars at auction, considering this one is a one-off, bodied in France, and designed by one of the most influential designers of the 20th Century, I'd venture to say that you could start out the bidding at, say, $2 million and change….

Chapter 48
Janis Joplin's Ride
(1965 Porsche 356 1600 Cabriolet)
Psychedelic Porsche on four wheels

It was both a car and a work of art, once owned by Janis Joplin, a hard driving blues songstress from Port Arthur Texas who celebrated splitting from her original group, Big Brother and the Holding Company, and going solo by buying a Porsche 356.

Hers was used, because she bought it in 1968, when the last ones were built in '66 (but titled as 1965 models).

She took delivery of it in white.

The story is that one of her "roadies" the assistants that travel with a singer and set up the equipment at each performance, a fella named Dave Richards, painted it in the surrealistic theme that was popular among some rock singers at the time (the Beatles did that to their Phantom V Rolls) and a popular theme in

posters by Peter Max.

Dave Richards painted jellyfish and butterflies, grandiosely calling the theme the "history of the universe."

The singer drove it everywhere around San Francisco, where she lived, and fans would leave notes on it on how much they loved her music.

Well, whaddya'know, somebody loved the car a little too much and, while she was up on stage performing at some San Francisco club, they up and stole it. I don't have the details on whether the miscreant was caught, but he did a dastardly crime against the car and against art, y'might say, by disguising the car by painting it over with gray primer paint, no doubt from a spray can.

Well, the car was spotted anyway and recovered and the primer chemically removed to reveal the original psychedelic paint job.

The story is since the psychedelic paint job had been coated with a seal coat, the primer was cleaned off and it still looked like it when she first had it custom painted. Janis drove it to her final trip in 1970 to a West Hollywood motel where she died of complications from drugs at the age of 27.

The car was then left in the care of her manager, who loaned it to other artists he managed, and the car gradually got worn down to the nubs, you might say. But the family, back in Texas, began to fret that the manager was letting the car go to seed. They got it back and then, when there was a musical playing about Janis' life, they loaned the car as a prop. Two set decorators got ahold of some old pictures of the car in Janis' heyday and re-created the original paint scheme, more or less.

Then in 1995 the family loaned it to a rock and roll Hall of Fame museum in Cleveland which kept it indoors and that helped keep the legend of Janis alive. Ironically one of her biggest hit songs was entitled) *"Oh, Lord won't you buy me a Mercedes Benz."*

THE TIME TO BUY

The time to buy the car, if there was a time when it had the least value, was when the manager had it. There seems to be some debate as to who owned it then, but there seemed to be no demand for it and the craze for collecting 356 Porsches hadn't started yet. But once the car was in the Museum, more and more people became aware of it and, as often happens with cars owned by celebrities, it grew in value.

Now, as a fine artist myself, I can't quite buy the re-constructed paint job being the equal of the original. That's like saying if the Mona Lisa painting burns up, still leaving the canvas and someone repaints it using photos as a guide, it's as valuable as the same painting. But then I compared different pictures of Janis with the car, and even in the photos it's obvious the car had been partially repainted even when she owned it. So it was an evolving painting, ya'might say.

After it came out of the Museum but before the musical featuring the car would have been a second chance to buy it, but once the family consigned it to RM-Sothebys auction company, well, then it was world famous—a celebrity car to own.

Stories published before the auction thought it would go for $400K to $600K but the power of rock and roll is stronger than that. It was hammered down sold in RM-Sotheby's "Driven to Disruption" sale for $1.76 million on Dec. 10th, 2015.

Lesson learned? Entertainers like to celebrate life, perhaps more than most of us. As a barn finder, it's your duty to start a file folder and list every entertainer who is pictured driving an interesting car, from Beyonce's Silver Cloud drophead to Rod Stewart's Lambos. And then, as the entertainer's star fades, as some of them inevitably do, you keep records on where the toys went. Hey, odds are they probably lost interest in some of them a long time ago and there's a right time to buy, *before* any of them hit the big time auction circuit.

Chapter 49
The Only American Pantera Speciale (1974 DeTomaso Pantera)

Just when you think it's verboten to import the European models, you discover the power of executive privilege...

In Italy there is a word for "custom" which, when applied to an automaker, means a car different from the others, usually ordered by a special VIP customer. The word is "speciale," pronounced "*spesch-ee-al*."

In this case, the VIP worked for Ford, and was the right hand man of Lee Iacocca. Most everyone remembers how Iacocca, while at Ford, was always trying to duplicate his former success tying Ford in with Carroll Shelby, putting Shel's Cobras into Ford showrooms, ordering up the Shelby Mustang, and sponsoring the creation of the Ford GT and its successful LeMans racing effort.

The DeTomaso tie-in was a lot smaller in scope. That deal came about when Henry Ford II, CEO and heir to a good bit of the family stock, got it in his head that everything Italian was wonderful. He divorced his American wife and married a blonde Italian divorcee. He tried to buy Ferrari and failed (that's how the GT40 was born—to spite Ferrari). A few years later, he again decided he wanted to tie in with an exotic Italian carmaker, but only if they would use Ford engines.

And so it was he courted DeTomaso, an irrepressible Argentine making cars in Italy and getting a lot of ink for a sexy, two-seat hot potato called the Mangusta. But HFII sent some minions to inspect the Mangusta, and discovered it was not fully developed and would be hard to build en masse. Before his minions left Modena, though, DeTomaso sold them on his next Ford-V8-powered mid-engine sports car, the Pantera, even though it only existed as a one-fifth-scale wood carving created by Tom Tjaarda, an American designer working in Italy for Ghia.

Ford ordered over 6,000 Panteras imported to America (sold at Lincoln-Mercury dealers), but they were as alike as peas in a pod, due to various laws forbidding American importers from customizing cars for wealthy customers as DeTomaso could in Italy. No bespoke spoken here, ya'might say.

THE BOSS'S RIGHT-HAND MAN PUTS IN AN ORDER

There's rules, and then there's rules. Despite the guvmint telling Ford what cars it could bring in and how it could sell them, there was a loophole through which Ford could bring in cars that didn't meet the specs: for evaluation by engineering or styling. Technically, these non-conforming cars are supposed to be sent back out of the country after evaluation, but one particular Pantera, Chassis No. THPNMD04275, somehow went up for sale.

Trying to find the car's history is a bit sketchy. It is listed as a 1974 DeTomaso Pantera GTS, but dig deeper and you'll find it was special-ordered by Ford Technical Director Hank Carlini back in 1972. That might have helped it squeak past the rules, as the '74 models imported to the US were the rubber-front-bumper L models.

At any rate, Carlini, who was serving as head coordinator between Ford, Ghia, and Vignale between 1971 and 1974, was perfectly placed to exert what we'll call executive privilege: he could order a car modified to his taste and oversee the build. In this case, he ordered a Euro-tuned engine, which had high compression. On the exterior it had unique hood vents, GTS wheel-arch flares, and F-O-R-D script on the rear deck lid—the same as the street-spec GT40. One report says a later owner was Charlene Ford—yes of the Ford family—who had the GTS lettering on the windshield and rockers removed because it looked tacky.

Historically the car is significant because it predates the American GTS by one year.

The car was offered in an auction on the website *Bring a Trailer.com.* There were a lot of pictures and copy that said "a magnet would stick almost everywhere" except for one four-inch-square section.

The interior, unlike the one-color interiors of American-market Panteras, boasted two-tone leather upholstery, a GTS clock, a Euro-spec radio, and a Momo Prototipo steering wheel with a Ghia center emblem instead of the stupid American-style wheel forced on all the other imported Panteras.

The ad offering the car on BringaTrailer.com said it had originally been fitted with a standard U.S.-market 8.6:1-compression 351C, then it got a European-spec 11:1-compression 380-horsepower version of Ford's Cleveland V-8. So, while "non-matching numbers" is a downgrade in value in car-collector circles, if the engine was replaced by the automaker before the car left the factory, well, that absolves the sin in my book.

The car was advertised in 2015 with 22,300 miles from new and had an aftermarket air cleaner and rocker covers fitted, though the originals were included. The ad was honest in stating minor flaws, like "a small main seal leak will need to be tended to."

The ad even showed a video of the car on a lift.

The car sold to a buyer from Switzerland in the early part of 2015. Apparently, it sold for between $74,500 and $76,000. One comment posted by a website reader after the sale said the buyer could turn around and sell it for twice the price. Well bought, I'd say!

Lesson learned? Okay, we know there are laws and U.S. customs regulations and the damn EPA and DOT and God knows what trying to prevent you from buying what you want, but the fact is that sometimes non-conforming foreign cars do come into the U.S. And sometimes they get offered for sale.

You have to rid your brain of the doctrinarian misconception that it is impossible to break the rules. When you are a high muckity-muck at an automaker, it's one of the perks—you can sometimes have a car built your way. It has been so since the dawn of the auto industry.

So the lesson is: if you hear of an executive having ordered a special car, a *Speciale* as the Italians say, try to track it down. Oft times, people lose interest in one car after ordering something newer, so the older *Speciale* gets sold.

In this case, whoever bought the old *Speciale* bought one of the few Panteras that's legal in America yet is different from all the rest—a documented factory *Speciale*.

Chapter 50

That Porsche Race Car That Got Away (1963 Porsche 356B Carrera 2000 GS/GT)

One thing you can count on with racers, their loyalty to their present ride is thin...

You go to the Porsche Museum in Stuttgart, and you see lots of rare cars, and you lament, "How can I find a really rare one? They've all been found."

Uh, not quite.

This is the story of a rare Porsche, one of two made. While one occupies a pride of place in the Museum, the other was lost for decades until re-discovered. Called the "three-pointed scraper" after a tool that clay modelers use, it's a model based on the 356B that came between the Carrera Abarths and preceded the mid-engine 904GTS.

The car came about when "Butzi" Porsche, grandson of Ferdinand, the firm's founder, wanted to make a more aerodynamic Porsche for testing the Carrera engine in racing. Porsche made two and, through a fluke in the rules, was allowed to enter them in the production classes.

They were successful in racing. But Porsche didn't want to make any more than two because, after all, the next big push was going to be the mid-engine 904GTS, and this three-pointed scraper was naught but a mule.

THE PORTUGESE CONNECTON

Now it happened that, at the time,there was in Portugal an accomplished driver, Americo Nunes. He was associated with the Portuguese Porsche distributor, for whom he was a jack-of-all-trades, doing everything from bodywork to sales. Through that connection, Nunes was able to persuade Porsche to sell him one of the two three-pointed scrapers when it was no longer useful to Porsche as a race car. It is difficult to tell which of the two he had, because authors quoting the chassis numbers often confuse the two.

According to Portuguese author Ricardo Grilo,

"In my opinion, Nunes' chassis number was 122 992and his German license plate was S-RS 262. I've seen many photos from both cars and the first one to race was the car with the large B pillar. And for me, that first Porsche Carrera GS/GT was #122 991 Nunes' Carrera GS/GT was the car with the narrower B pillar and through pictures it is easy to follow both cars in their racing careers. Some authors ignored the different B pillars of each car and arbitrarily assign them different chassis numbers in different races, paying no attention to the details that distinguish the two cars."

Nunes bought the race car in June or July of 1965 and drove it from Zuffenhausen to Portugal by road in an epic 36-hour, non-stop flog, just in time to make his racing debut with the car at the Cascais circuit. Nunes was forced to retire when a Lotus Elan collided with his new Porsche.

For Nunes, a hands-on kinda guy,this was not a real problem. He had always disliked the rear of the car so, being a bodywork expert, he redesigned the rear according to his own aesthetic standards, borrowing more than a little from the new 904GTS with its "sugar scoop" rear window. All this bodywork was done in record time as he and his friend, Evaristo Saraiva, had already entered the car in the Spanish Rias Bajas Rally, to be held only two weeks after their race at Cascais!

Not only was the car ready in time to go to Spain, it won the race. It was a real feather in Nunes' and Saraiva's caps, winning a rally with a car that had run at LeMans. Two weeks later, Nunes drove the Carrera 2000 GS/GT to a good second-place overall at Vila do Conde Circuit, near Porto. The winner was a much more powerful Ferrari 275 GTB. Nunes was doing so well, he added a second Porsche, a 356 SC, and continued to race both cars at every kind of event possible.

In 1966, Nunes again modified the rear of his Carrera 2000 GS/GT, this time going more to a design similar to the Carrera Abarth. With this new look, it participated in some 1966 Portuguese Driver's Championship events. But unlike his very solid and dependable 356 SC, the Carrera 2000 GS/GT was a very difficult car to keep running.

A PICKLE IN PARIS

The sad part of the story begins here, get out your hankerchief. Nunes set out on a trip to Zuffenhausen— where Porsches are made, to get some work done on the car; his longer-range plan being to exchange it for a second-hand, ex-factory 911.

On the way, passing through Paris, he blew the engine. Now, four-cam Carrera engines are so rare that there were probably no parts or engine builders in Paris he trusted. So what does Nunes do? He sells it to a French junk dealer in Paris.

Here comes the part that hurts to even tell about it. What did he get for this one-off (well, two-off, technically), four-cam, factory race car? I hate to even print it—about $200, just enough to catch the next one-way flight back to Portugal.

Now comes the part that even hurts to tell about. How much did he sell this one-off (well, two-off, technically) 4-cam factory race car for? I hate to even print it—about $200—just enough to catch the next one-way flight back to Portugal.

Today that car is worth a million dollars.

(Excuse my tears staining this page)

BRIEF HOPE DASHED

I had a moment that comes to every barn finder—when you hear a rumor that may have some basis in truth. The rumor was that the car was in Northern California.

Which it was, for a time

But my hopes of finding it in a barn covered with dust owned by some rube who had ought a "furrin" car" and then didn't know where to get it fixed were dashed as I did more research, writing the Portugese Porsche 356 club for more clues.

Alas, my hopes were dashed again when they reported that it went from the French junkyard to Frenchman Michael Tassy, and from there in 1987 to a real French connoisseur of Porsche four-cams (he already owned three of them) Andre Pibarot. Pibarot restored the car to its original "three pointed scraper" look, though he had to go by pictures, there being no factory body panels available. He and his son entered it in vintage rallies.

He must have found another Porsche he loved more and sold it to a new owner in the U.S. in 2003, Doctor Julio Palmez, a prominent Porsche collector (whose race cars can be seen in his private museum if you go on a tour of his winery in Napa,CA). In 2015, Dr. Palmez sold it to a Swedish gentleman.

There's lessons aplenty here for barn hunters. First, and write this on the inside of your eyelids so you won't forget it—racers, not vintage racers, but those racing current cars, only think of the next race car they are going to get. Nunes knew Porsche would give him a sweet deal on a racing 911 so he thought "easy come, easy go," and dumped the broken 4-cam 356B so he could work on getting a 911. And, he did indeed win many races in 911 Porsches, in both rallying and on racing circuits and died very recently at a ripe old age in his '80s.

So stick close to racers, your checkbook in hand. Monitor

their progress or lack of it. If they see a chance to jump out of an obsolete car into one that's new-new-new, you know they'll do it and this is where you step in to buy the "left-over," hopefully with damage as minimal as a piston through the block.

So the "window of opportunity" to buy this car at a bargain price was exceedingly small, really only when it was in the junkyard. Which is, by the way, one reason that, when you are in a new city as a tourist, you should bargain with your wife to let you tour a junkyard or two.

Once it left the junkyard, and got into the hands of a noted 4-cam collector, it was "anointed with gold" you could say because, the reasoning being among collectors, "If Andre has it, it is worth collecting."

Another lesson, though, is that car factories are run by, dare we say, merchants. Yes, some of them love cars, but the objective —to their stockholders anyway— is to make a profit. And to do that, you have to sell cars. So it is that, throughout this series, I tell again and again of how a factory sells a car that they really should keep around for posterity. Your job as a barn finder is to keep track of the disposition of rare and one-off models in case the factory pushes yet another one toward the door.

Hopefully, when they do, you'll be there to take it off their hands...

IN SUM

So there you have it, barn finders. 50 stories and almost 50 ways to find a rare collectable car.

If you have another few minutes, here's some observations based on what's in this book and the previous three volumes (see Enthusiast Books' website to add those to your library).

ALWAYS BE LOOKING

In the sales world there is a saying something like "always be closing." Well, it's the same thing in the barn find world. Even if you are on the way to grandma's house with the kids, have a digital camera with you and, if you spot an interesting car in a driveway or garage, pull over and shoot a couple pictures from the curb, then shoot a picture of the house number and then the street sign so you can find that address again should the car be of interest to you later. And even if not you, maybe it will be of interest to a dealer (read on to find out how to merchandise your info).

USING NEW TECHNOLOGY

I carry a couple of Canon A2300 digital PowerShot cameras which run about $60 each at a pawnshop (less on eBay). With a 16MB memory card they will take over one thousand pictures per card. That's a phenomenal amount of pictures, so best to periodically sit down and download the accrued images onto your office computer hard drive lest you lose the camera or memory card.

Let me give you an example of how I shot a car on the fly so to speak. I am driving through Chino, CA , coming from an early morning feed at the ranch (I am a cowpoke in my other life) and I see a lot of tent roof covers (without sides) in a guy's yard. The kind of tents that cover cars. I pull over onto a side street and he's got beaucoup covering on the chain link fence, to prevent prying eyes. But I am out on the street, so figure I'm on

Record all sightings on digital camera & save to your hard drive on home computer when you get home in a "Future Prospect" file. I passed this Ghia and it only took 5 seconds to stop, shoot the car and record the street name and house number so I can contact the owner later. Year from now I could write a postcard and ask if it's for sale.

public property (that I pay for as a taxpayer) So from the street I shoot into the yard through the chain link fence and there's barely a fender visible of one of the cars he has under the tents and tarps. It's a fender from a '63 through '67 Corvette.

Next, once I am at the office, I go to Google.com and type in the guy's address, and select an aerial view, Google Satellite. Alas, you see the tents but can't make out any cars.

Stage 3. I write the house owner a postcard. Now, if there's ever any time that success or failure depends on every single word being right, this is it. The postcard should be hand written, God knows you don't want the owner to think you pitch lots of car owners and carry around pre- printed cars. And you don't let on you are a frequent buyer; strike a tone that's more an "Aw Shucks" approach like "I was passin' by and I thought I saw a Corvette" and then add that it's always been your dream, yadda yadda.

I got no answer.

No biggie. I moved on, with those pictures in my file. I might wait for one of those days when the winds are 70 mph and see if the tarp blows off the Vette. Why does it matter? We're talking dollars here, big ones. It is very significant regarding value to determine whether it is a big block or a small block. A 427 '67 would be worth twice what a '63 small block 327 would be worth. An L88 427 (they only made 20 or so in the '67 model year) would be worth close to a million if it was numbers matching engine-to-chassis in the factory records. So that Corvette is on my check-back-periodically list (I am reminded of the late car historian Len Frank, who when visited in San Pedro, by LA harbor, would take friends on a tour of "cars on his watch list."

MARKETING YOUR INFO

Now let's say you are a car enthusiast just steeped in information, right up to your eyeballs. You can walk through a car show with a less educated friend and point out this car or that and say things like "That's a 396 big block Corvette, they made those before the 427, yadda-yadda." But let's say that, at the present moment you don't have any money stashed in your cookie jar. That does not mean that the information you come across is useless. Far from it.

There are barn finders in the big leagues, guys who travel all over the world bagging cars that might sell for a million, who will reward you if you find a valuable car.

THE INTERNET—IT'S YOUR FRIEND *AND* YOUR ENEMY

Now the problem is that, since the internet came into virtually every home, keeping a barn find car's location secret is a huge problem. In the days of film cameras (remember them?) I would shoot snapshots and send them to interested collectors and they would leisurely send me back letters or maybe a cashier's check to go out and buy it for them. Well, now information dissemination is instantaneous.

For example, I was driving through San Bernardino and I saw a Jaguar XKE poking its snout out of a car upholsterer's shop. I stopped and talked to a shop employee and he said "there's two of them here, both here for storage." Now I don't want to knock a town's reputation, but San Bernardino is not in the chips. The Mayor was once quoted as saying the town was "in free fall." So that means these cars might have been spotted by a lot of passersby but few have the moola to buy them. So they could still be there. I didn't get enough info—whether they are coupes, or roadsters, early or late, but any E-type is worth at least $50,000 if a dime. So that's another one that needs the postcard treatment, and maybe some pre-marketing to dealers with a picture.

OPERATIONAL SECURITY

In order not to totally waste your barn finding efforts, you have to come to grips with the necessity of keeping the information relatively secret. If I shot these cars, those Jags, for instance, I would shoot around the license plates and wouldn't give any dealers I sent the pictures to a clue as to where they were. Of course they know I am in Southern California because that's where I am writing from but the pictures would not have a sign visible like "Joes' Garage." In fact you have to be careful not to even show the cars in the background. In one case I found a '39 Bentley sedanca de ville but, in the background, there were a bunch of Italian cars, all the same model, same brand so it would be easy for a cagey dealer to go on the web and ask owners of that Italian car: "Who's a guy in So Cal who has three of those cars, two of them smashed?" Once he found that name, he would know where the Bentley is.

The SN is the most important. If you give that away early on to potential buyers of the information, you've compromised your operational security. In the case of the Bentley, I gave the SN to a British writer and a couple days later he e-mailed me, with the owner's name, so, while I love the internet for the information so immediately on tap, if you don't properly hide where the car you barn found is, you are just giving the information away. In the case of the Bentley, I drove one hour across LA in rush hour traffic, plus an hour back and so there's gas, meals and the research I did on the car later. I'm not giving away that information, much as I would like to be congratulated by Bentley buffs on finding a treasure.

Last year I sold information on two collections. One was a collection of 35 RRs and Bentleys. That was one where the cars weren't actually for sale when I photographed them, but the owner just wanted it to be known that he had a collection. He used the cars quite a lot in publicity for his chain of exercise parlors. I went out there, shot the pictures, wrote a description and that packet was offered to various car dealers in the US and UK. Some dealers even accused me of being a scam artist, to which I took exception, being a historian. (Once the cars are sold I might send them the newspaper clipping to show them the collection existed). I sold the packet for about $250. Now you could say, why not let the car dealer pay you a commission for each car he buys?" The dealers would offer me that. But I thought "that's all well and good but I'd rather have a bit of change now." That way I don't have to periodically check "Did you buy one of the cars yet?"

A MUSEUM UP FOR GRABS

The second sale of an information packet resulted from a tour or a museum. I knew the youngish owner had died recently so when I concluded my tour, I asked the docent "What's happening with all these cars?" He shrugged and said 'It's in the courts."

So I contacted dealers far and wide and one was willing to pony up for pictures and my estimate of who to reach in the fight for assets to make a pitch for buying the cars. I sold that packet for a few hundred to a big classic car dealer and threw in the advice to follow the example of those antique hunters on

TV--buy anything, any one object, for an exaggerated price, to show them you are good for the money, and then they will take you seriously. But I don't think he took my advice, as I later saw the same cars at auction.

DON'T TAKE FRIENDS WITH YOU TO LOOK AT CARS

Now time was I would go look at a car with a car buddy, but I can tell you here and now that's not a good idea. My most sterling example was when I found an Iso Grifo near my house when I lived out by LAX airport. It has a silver leather interior, an unusual color to be sure (I had previously only seen that on GM show cars during the Bill Mitchell era). I went with a friend that was in the same Iso car club as I. We wrote down the owner's information and a few weeks later my customer in New York said "Go get that car" and I had lost the information. I called up my "friend" (and you will soon see why there's quotation marks around "friend" soon) and he denied he had ever gone to view the car. This in spite of the fact he had brought a friend with him so there was a witness. Someday I will find the history of the silver leather-equipped Grifo coupe and know he brokered it behind my back. There is simply no other explanation. He had brokered it and didn't want to share the commission.

CARS 'N COFFEE

Early bird gets the worm and all that, right? Well, now that there are "Cars 'n Coffee" meets everywhere, which are basically informal car shows in a parking lot where you "run what you brung." It pays to get up out of bed on these days and go to these because there is always the possibility people will show up who have no clue what their car is presently worth on today's market. I have been to three Supercar Sundays in Agoura recently (a name a sponsoring car dealer gives to their "Cars 'n Coffee")and each time I saw a rare car with an owner who didn't look that up on the recent selling prices. In fact one old couple with a Porsche 356 pre-A coupe admitted they didn't know how to use the internet. Contrast that with those slicksters who pull out an I-phone, zip through some files and announce "Yes, at the last Gooding auction at Monterey one of those went for $245,000."

I admit when I go to these car shows I don't always have notebooks to take notes. You really need that, the old fashioned kind of notes, pen and paper. Get them to write their name, and phone number and e-mail. But don't act too eager to buy their car, it's only a sort of "let me see if these cars are popular," something vague. And take pictures. As I said, my camera will take over 1000 pictures on a 16 GB memory card. And a new memory card is, what, $12!

BE A WORLD CLASS SCHMOOZER

When researching the chapter on the search for the James Dean Speedster, I wrote up what I knew about the car, and sent a story on it to a couple of 356 clubs as far as Australia. I was not looking to get paid, I mean how much can a club pay a correspondent, right? But I was hoping, later on down the road, when I am working on my 356 book (Porsche 356 Photo Album, due in 2017) someone in one of those clubs might read the manuscript, or somesuch, and volunteer a golden nugget of information. Well what'd'ya know, someone from the 356 club de France says "We have a club member who owns that car." I was flabbergasted, as a writer who is obsessed with James Dean told me he has been looking for it for several decades. So my recommendation is, when you go to an event, shoot pictures, take notes on the event overall and send a packet of information on the event to a club dealing in that model, or at least that marque.

Then when you go to that foreign country, I guarantee you that you will know somebody there to have a cuppa java with and who might show you cars in that country or introduce you to engine builders, restorers, etc. Now I know guys who can't be bothered to send a picture with no possibility of being paid, but I say nothing ventured, nothing gained. Wasn't there some sort of movement awhile back called "Pay it forwards,' where you do a favor for someone and maybe they'll do one for you or someone else?

THE GARAGE OWNER IS YOUR FRIEND

In one of the earlier volumes in this series I told of my long time friendship with a garage owner, Al Axelrod, who worked in West Hollywood on a lot of celebrity owned cars. (He turned away Steve McQueen because McQueen wanted him to work on his cars for free, for the publicity). Anyhow, in that book I tell of the Ferrari 365GTC/4 I found in the shop. Al was trying to buy it but failed. Later on I saw the same car on a used car lot and found the owner's registration in the glove compartment. Since I knew what price Al had offered, I knew what to offer myself, and got the car.

So I say if you are specializing in a particular brand of car, be it Boss Mustangs or Porsche 356 cars, you should make it a habit to drop by a garage that specializes in the model you like.

Pass by often, and get to know the owner. Maybe you have a stack of old club magazine that he would like to go through. Maybe you shot detailed pictures of a restored car of the same type he works on and he will be grateful to show his customer "this is the way we should finish the engine," etc.

If it's a hot day, bring a cold beer. If it's a cold day, bring warm donuts.

SPREAD THE WORD YOU ARE LOOKING

The best story I know of about spreading the word is a colleague of mine. He was struck with the beauty of the Bizzarrini GT5300 Strada while still in high school. He must have waxed eloquent about it because, years later, a high school girl he had gone to school with called him and said "Hey, you still crazy about that Bitz-0-reen-E (that's how she pronounced it)?" He said "Yes" and she said "There's one here for sale" and he rushed over and bought it for peanuts. Unfortunately he never restored it but he still has it 30-40 years later, so thank goodness he let everybody know what car he liked. Somebody remembered his passion.

One way to do that is print business cards picturing your dream car, be it a '37 Ford, a Rolls Royce Silver Cloud, whatever. Say "Such and such car wanted" and promise a reward.

Now those rewards could be contingent on if you get the car, but not necessarily. If I were looking for say, a rare car, I'd be grateful for any information on where one is, even if I don't' get the card, the owner at the time you look at it might not be interested in selling but peoples lives change. The need comes up. They get married, join the Army, get busted on a DUI, get sick, have accidents, sometimes even die.

But the cars just sit there, they don't know what's happening until the new owner shows up.

The best example of that is the Cobra Daytona coupe. This barn finder from England found the lady that owned it (and who had refused to sell it for decades, even turning down Carroll Shelby). He wrote her a nice letter but the lady died (ruled a suicide) and her elderly mother finds the letter in her daughter's papers, calls up the dealer and the deal went through --$3 million. He sold it the next day for $4 million.

That barn finder never would have gotten the car if he hadn't written the letter.

THE CLUB SCENE

Now some might feel that joining a car club is the last place you will find a valuable car at a bargain price because everybody in the club knows what they are worth. Well, there's two ways to look at that. Sometimes club members buy beyond their budget. They go ga-ga and buy a couple of project cars and to complete both of them at the same time is eating them out of house and home. I remember, I wasn't even a member of a RR or Bentley club when some member meeting me at a RR meeting said "I have a James Young bodied Mk. VI at my house, you want to look at it? " I did and it was a genuine coachbuilt car. Very rough. The reason he was selling it is that he was knee deep in doing an even rarer car so he offered the Bentley to me for $4,000. Probably worth about $140,000 now. Nobody in his club wanted it at the time and he needed to get it out of the driveway so he made the offer. He wouldn't have met me if I hadn't gone to a club meeting.

THE HUNT ABROAD

One of the classic lines in American literature is a character Ben in Arthur Miller's *Death of a Salesman*. He says something like "Why, boys, when I was seventeen I walked *into the jungle* and when I was twenty-one I walked *out*, and by God I was *rich*! "

We all that fantasy that you can go to a foreign country, and the rubes over there won't know the value of that old car you find, and sell it cheap. Well, I am here to tell ya that the cars are over there, I've seen them—a Bizzarrini in Holland, a gullwing Mercedes in Manila—most of the time the people who own valuable cars in foreign countries know precisely what they are worth.

Still, sometimes they are in a quandary. Especially if they are on an island. I remember when there was a car on some small Hawaiian island and nobody wanted to buy a GTO-nosed Lusso Ferrari. Then they are faced with shipping it to another island, or the mainland. What if the engine is broken? Then on their little island they have to find a Ferrari mechanic. That's why a car might be sitting for decades. No parts there. No me-

Always have your camera ready. I carry a digital camera at all times. When I was touring a collection in storage and saw this prewar Bentley sedanca de ville, I shot a picture and recorded the owner info. I can't afford it myself but it's information to market to a collector I haven't met yet.

chanics that can fix the car. And no buyer for the car.

I have yet another example. This Doctor in Canada had occasion to land his small plane on a small island. He sees a gullwing Mercedes sitting in a hanger at the airport. He finds out the car is owned by an island local, who rarely drives it. Who, among all of the world's gullwing fans, would think there was one on this tiny island? No one. He got it, not at a bargain find price (under a million anyway).

The downside of this fantasy is that, once you are outside the U.S. and Canada, and Western Europe, in third world countries, there is a power elite who want to be cut into every deal, and if you don't know anyone in the power elite you are more or less unprotected in making your purchase. You might buy the car only to find out once you get to the docks or airport with the car that you didn't know what a proper title looks like in that country or how to find out who the real owner is. And let's say you make it to the airport with your treasure to fly it out. Their version of customs might say it lacks the proper paperwork and there's no native of that country who you can get to act as your ombudsman to get it straightened out. Not to say it can't happen,

I went up to Toronto Canada in the mid-'60s and bought

CONSIDER A NON-U.S-SPEC MODEL. By buying a car that was never officially imported by the automaker, you automatically have a rare car, that is worth more than U.S. models. But you'll have to order parts overseas. Fortunately this one had an engine in common with approved U.S. models. But be sure somebody else has gone through registration problems and it is already has plates form one of the 50 U.S. states. like this Alfa Junior Zagato.

a Mercedes gullwing, and even though the owner gave me the wrong title (wouldn't 'cha know he had two of them) but I still got it into the US in those pre-computer days as they looked at it as a typing error. But Canada is lot like the US, not a third world country filled with intrigues and friends of the local dictator.

The biggest revelation I had doing this fourth volume in the *Incredible Barn Finds* quartet is that some of the most valuable cars existed for a time with the wrong bodywork on them. There's many reasons for the body change. Oh, some dude thought he was a better designer than the original designer and had his way with the sheet metal. Or worse, some fool crashed it and a body of another far or a makeshift body was installed. I think of how many times I have been at a race and saw an ugly race car, obviously homebuilt and failed to walk over and ask "and what chassis is under that car?" Coulda been a diamond disguised as a rhinestone as the Ferrari F1 in this book was, a two seater wanna be GTO body installed on a single seater.

And so it is, I hope this fourth batch of stories from the front lines of car collecting have inspired you enough to tell the naysayers to take a hike. Those who want to rain on your parade have one favorite mantra: "It's no use looking—they've all been found."

Not true. I run across collector cars about once a week just toodling about.

I've enjoyed the collector cars I had much more than the cars I bought new, partly because I had pride in the way I found them. I hope in a future book in this series I'll be writing about the adventure *you* had in making your making your barn find.... Good hunting!

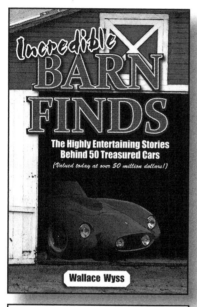
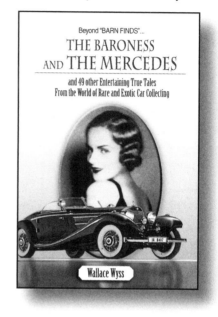